CW00496892

THE AMBASSADOR

KINGDOM LIFE IN THE HERE AND NOW

MANDY CARR

ISBN-13 (print edition): 979-8-37676-482-4

*To all the Church Family at St. George's, Sevenoaks
Weald*

With love and gratitude

***

*'I thank my God every time I remember you. In all my
prayers for all of you, I always pray with joy because of
your partnership in the gospel from the first day until
now, being confident of this, that He who began a good
work in you will carry it on to completion until the day of
Christ Jesus.'*

Philippians 1: 3-6 (NIV)

CONTENTS

Foreword   vii

Prologue   1
Introduction - Building A Bridge As
We Walk Across It   3
1. In Search Of The Kingdom   11
2. Dethroning Caesar   22
3. Union   32
4. Relapse   48
5. Partners in Borrowed Shoes   54
6. Unfinished Business   60
7. Offence   73
8. Blessing   85
9. Course Correction   97
10. Gordian Knots   115
11. The Question Of Power   131
12. Communication With HQ   147
13. Kingdom Values   165
14. The Practice Of Proclamation   182
15. Re-Wiring Required   200
16. The Seal Of The Lamb   215
17. Working From Rest   225
18. Living Inside Out For Others   242
Epilogue - The Rope Swing At The
End Of The Bridge   257

Notes   267
Acknowledgments   285
About the Author   287
Also by Mandy Carr   289

FOREWORD

Every time I typed FOREWORD the autocorrect decided to write FIREWORD. As I thought about it "FIREWORD" describes this latest book from Mandy. It follows her epic encounters on the beach with the Divine Trinity and its resulting reflection, study and prayer work.

Now, in *The Ambassador*, Mandy is led to explore identity, vocation and what on earth the Kingdom of God coming where you live is all about.

Its wide-ranging theology and encounters with neuroscience and, believe it or not, quantum physics, work together to reveal the wholeness of Creator God's work.

Having said that, this is not a staid book of information but a written encounter of what it is like, that is to say, the lived experience when you allow God to direct your thinking, your prayer and your wondering.

So, there is no finely crafted outline, no predetermined progress between chapters but the story of risk. Alongside it, you will find the invitation to travel with Mandy on this fruitful exploration of what it means to be a beloved child of God.

While we will all have our own journeys, in this book you will discover points at which you will find yourself pausing, questioning, wondering and even being disturbed by what you read. At times it will be challenging, as it was for me.

Perhaps the biggest challenge for all of us is what we will allow God to do in our lives with these challenges, these moments of pausing, wondering and what the next part of the book of your life will hold.

Be blessed with this book and the presence of the Divine Trinity.

Jean Kerr
    February 2023

PROLOGUE

AMBASSADOR 1. An accredited diplomat sent by a State on a mission to, or as its permanent representative in, a foreign country. 2. A representative or promoter of a specified thing *(an ambassador of peace.)* [1]

A Prophetic Word from 24.12.21

"I am taking you into a new season where I am going to build on the identity I've spoken about. That truth was who you are; now I'm going to share who I am in you. It is this Divine union that gives you your power and authority. I am with you, and I am within you. Everything that is said about Me is true for you, because I dwell in you and you in Me. Speak it out as a word of faith and it will come about. Speak out My heart as the present continuous tense and My kingdom will be estab-

lished in that moment. I cannot speak falsehood. I cannot speak against Myself.

What you carry is dynamite resurrection power. The last season was about you and My love for you. This season is about that love at work through you for all humankind. I'm taking you into a place of stability and security, established with Me. It is not what you have done; it is what I have done in you, and what I'm going to do in and through you.

I'm going to give you faith to see My kingdom come and My will to be done. You're going to live inside-out.

Work with Me, move with Me. Encourage yourself with the truth of God. Reach out to My heart and live from it, not for it. It has already been established. I'm looking for lovers who will love well, know My truth in every situation and steward My gift within. This is about Me within.

Make room for your king and learn to represent Me as My Ambassador. I have called you into this role. This means you know what powers you have because you represent Me. Everywhere you place your foot is holy ground because I am within you. Learn to speak My word."

INTRODUCTION - BUILDING A BRIDGE AS WE WALK ACROSS IT

'To be an ambassador for Christ means to invite everyone to a personal encounter with Jesus'

Pope Francis

'The words 'to be continued...' are ever present because that is the nature of our spiritual lives.'

The Ambassador

I started writing this book not knowing where I was going. I am therefore writing this introduction now I have had an opportunity to reflect on the journey. I have learned a lot through the process and one of those things is that God calls us to be present *now*, to respond to Him *now*, and to be willing to divert our course if He tells us. Constant communication that involves waiting for Him to speak to us is essential, otherwise we can easily feel that there is no difference between our best laid plans and the purposes of God. Keeping short accounts helps this. We come to God for answers to our questions, direction, clarification, and review, always willing to be open to surprises and changes in plan.

Writing this book in the aftermath of the Covid-19 pandemic has underlined this. This global experience has been a great disrupter of our pattern of life and brought huge loss in its wake. It has also created change. The enforced restrictions brought on by the pandemic have given us permission to stop those things in our culture or tradition that we couldn't sustain or had outlasted their usefulness, and it has pushed us to develop and transform ourselves in ways we hadn't considered. Some of this has been very painful, but in other ways it has been creative and energising. It has forced a season of liminality upon us. The author, Susan Beaumont, describing this transitional experience, writes:

'During liminal seasons we stand on both sides of a threshold. We have one foot rooted in something that is not yet over, whereas the other foot is planted in a thing not yet defined, something not ready to begin. Our old operating structures may no longer work.[1]

Although this throws up many challenges, Beaumont argues that God's greatest work occurs in liminal space.[2] I recognised the reality of this during lockdown periods where I had a series of dreams and encounters with God that I describe in my previous book, *The Beach.* It changed me, inviting me to think about Father, Son, and Holy Spirit in a new way. I grew in intimacy with God as I also learned about His love, grace, and playfulness. Our time together taught me to inhabit my role of being a child of God who is loved just as I am.

It also challenged me on many levels, particularly about the place of pain in our lives and what makes us continue to trust in God's mercy and goodness when faced with suffering. I wrote about my history of severe and chronic migraines and my discussions with God about them. I went on a journey of learning about the emotional factors that contribute to neuroplastic pain, such as fear and trauma. Within a loving relationship with God, I learned how to begin to tackle them.

Over time, my migraines have lessened in intensity but they have not disappeared completely. I do not see the lack of cure as a failure on mine or God's part. I still hold out for complete healing but recognise that sometimes this comes through a process, rather than a single event. God taught me so much in this past season, but I know the story is not over. *The Ambassador* leads on from where my previous book ended.

In the Epilogue of *The Beach*, I recounted a dream and the last line read:

'It's now time to go out into the darkness and be His light.' [3]

This conclusion felt prophetic. God was calling me into a different phase of life, but I didn't know what that meant. The lack of clarity made me uneasy as I felt both the weightiness of the words, and my inability to grasp their meaning. Over time, however, I began to be stalked by the theme of being an ambassador for Christ. It turned up everywhere in what I read and watched, which was a sure sign that God was trying to get my attention and He wasn't being subtle. The Apostle Paul's second letter to the church in Corinth introduces us to the concept of being ambassadors. He writes:

'We are therefore Christ's ambassadors, as though God were making his appeal through us. We implore you on Christ's behalf: be reconciled to God. God made him who had no sin to be sin for us, so that in him we might become the righteousness of God.' [4]

Paul urges the Church at Corinth to understand that something new has happened that affects everything. The death, resurrection and ascension of Jesus has precipitated this new beginning and life will never be the same again. They are now living in this new world and, as followers of Jesus, they are entrusted with the same message of reconciliation. Bishop Tom Wright states:

'The new world has a new king, and the king has ambassadors...[Paul] is going into all the world with a

*message from its newly enthroned sovereign, a message
inviting anyone and everyone to be reconciled to the God
who made them, loves them, and has provided the means
of reconciliation for them to come back to know and love
him in return.*'[5]

This book is an exploration of what it means to
be an ambassador for the Kingdom of God. The first
part is about personal formation, and the second
half is about kingdom culture, its values, power,
authority, and the transformation required.

Being an ambassador for Christ is a weighty
vocation and I quickly became aware of a yawning
chasm between this high calling and my own spiritual life. I couldn't see how I would be able to bridge
this gap and remain authentic, but Susan Beaumont
reminded me that this is also a symptom of transitional periods. She writes:

*'Liminal seasons require us to build the bridge as we
walk on it.'* [6]

While I initially talk in terms of *becoming* an
ambassador, I take a course correction later in the
book, realising that this is not quite accurate. I have
left it in, unedited, because each of the twists and
turns, backtracks, and sprints ahead are all part of
the same journey. It doesn't help others to give the
impression that the path must be smooth and trou-
ble-free when that isn't an accurate picture of most
people's experience.

As I look back on this last year, I realise that my

perception has shifted. It has been a Copernican Revolution. Peter Scazzero's books on emotional health within the church feature this shift of thinking. Copernicus in the 1500s, and later Galileo, challenged assumptions that the earth was the centre of the universe. They proposed, instead, that the earth was just one of the many planets that orbited the sun. This thinking was considered sacrilegious at the time and Galileo was accused of heresy by the Church. Peter Scazzero states:

'Today we still use the phrase Copernican revolution to describe a whole new way of looking at life, one that shakes the foundations of how we feel, think, or see something.' [7]

Writing about being an ambassador for Christ has shifted my thinking about the shape and focus of ministry. In Western Europe, where we are experiencing a decline in the number of those who identify as practising Christians, there is pressure on existing ministers and congregations to turn things around. Church hierarchies are urging us to follow strategies for growth and stretch resources further. Ill-health and burn out are more common, as well as low-grade depression in church leaders and their congregations, as we seek to stop people leaving the church and work hard to invite more members to join. Writing this book has re-focused my attention on seeking the kingdom rather than building the church. It has released me from the burden of thinking that, as a church leader, it's down to me and our congregation. This simply isn't true. This is about the completed work of Jesus. He has already done what is needed. We just get the privilege of being in partnership with Him and applying it in the now.

What follows is an exploration of what, I believe, it means to be an ambassador for Christ in the twenty-first Century. It's not an exhaustive study, it is a story of my journey and one which I hope will spur others on. We are all invited to consider what it means to be in union with the living God and to represent Him and His finished work in the world. Although this book relies more on scripture and reason than the imagination of *The Beach*, it builds on what went before and the experiences flow into one another. The words 'to be continued...' are ever present because that is the nature of our spiritual lives.

As I share this journey, I have the assurance that writing about being an ambassador for Christ is a call from Abba. He will lead me forward until I reach the next season and the narrative takes a different turn. It's that liminal space again, leading us onto new discoveries in God.

It is now time to build the bridge as I walk across it.

1

IN SEARCH OF THE KINGDOM

Its "present tense" existence was explained in Jesus' statement. "The kingdom of heaven is at hand." That means heaven is not just our eternal destination, but also is a present reality, and it's within arms reach.'

Bill Johnson

'To put it more simply, the power of the Spirit from God's glory realm breaks through into our timeline and changes matter – on earth as in heaven. This restructures the physical world according to the will of God. Heaven essentially invades earth.'

The Ambassador

When we talk about being an ambassador for

the Kingdom of God, we need to think about what the kingdom means. Can we define what we are talking about? And is it the same as how those in the first century in Galilee understood it? One place to start is looking at the historical understanding of the kingdom within Jewish culture.

The concept of *the kingdom* is multi-layered and coloured by Israel's history, culture, theology, and political ideology. From the time of the covenant made between God and Abraham, the people embraced a sense of destiny. From the Hebrew Scriptures we learn that God had chosen them as His people and they had been promised a land in which to settle.[1] In the story of the exodus, celebrated each year at Passover, they remember how God had delivered them from slavery in Egypt.[2] During the wilderness years, God led them through the desert by a pillar of cloud or fire[3] and fed them with manna.[4] On Mount Sinai Moses received the Ten Commandments and renewed the Covenant between God and the Israelites.[5] All of this history lived in their collective consciousness and God was understood literally as the king of Israel.[6] Judges and Prophets as God's representatives had led Israel until the people wanted to be like other nations and asked to have a king of their own.[7] This resulted in the anointing of Saul, who God later rejected as king,[8] followed by the popular kingship of David. However, David and his successors were unable to consolidate their power in a monarchy and the kingdom split into two parts.

By the time of Jesus, the people of the region had come under the rule of one empire after another and each time the occupation sparked rebellion and resistance. Donald Kraybill writes:

'...*various factors fuelled the public anger, including rural poverty, high taxes, Roman control, inflammatory acts of Jewish puppet kings, and the crushing violence of Roman armies. Political, economic, and religious factors combined together to stir revolt and rebellion. The slogan of many of the zealous resisters was "No Lord but God".'* [9]

Out of centuries of turmoil came the belief in an 'anointed one' or *Messiah*. This was a human being who would be called by God as king. The Messiah would usher in the age to come and through His chosen one, God would bring a new age of peace and prosperity. The Temple would be renewed and Israel's enemies would be defeated. Divine rule would be re-established.

Although there were diverse opinions about some of the details, the coming of the Messiah had been prophesied in the Hebrew Scriptures for centuries.[10] There was an expectation that a deliverer would arise to lead the people and throw off the yoke of tyranny, and this became a common theme for the oppressed to camp around. In the century before the destruction of the Temple in 70 C.E., there were seven major public protests, the emergence of ten prophets preaching deliverance (of which John the Baptist was just one), and five self-appointed messiahs, not including Jesus. This all reflected the widespread turbulence in the land[11] as well as the political dimension that the Kingdom of God had acquired, as the people looked back to Israel's freedom when God was king alone and yearned for it again.

While the appearance of the Messiah would be the sign that the kingdom was on its way, the problem was that Jesus didn't fit into the expected mould. It was an ongoing challenge to the crowds, the religious establishment, and to Jesus' inner circle, to discern who He was because of this disparity. He may have taught extensively about the kingdom, but He was a different kind of messiah, which meant that, for some, He was no messiah at all. While He may not have looked like the traditional deliverer of popular expectation, Nick Page's book, *The Wrong Messiah*, argues that Jesus fulfilled His mission in a better way, stating:

'He drove out the enemy, but the enemy proved to be not the Romans, but death. He renewed the temple, but the temple proved to be His body, rebuilt after three days. He brought in a new kingdom, but it was not a worldly kingdom, it was a kingdom of servanthood, of love, of peace. And it was never to end.' [12]

Jesus may have exemplified the kingdom through His life and teachings, but He also spoke about it in different ways, and this illustrated its complexity. Biblical scholar, Kenneth Bailey, explains this complexity in three paradoxes.[13] First, the Kingdom of God has *already come* in the person of Christ, but that same kingdom is still in the future. Secondly, the Kingdom of God is *near* and yet *far away*, and we can see Jesus using these terms of distance in the Gospels when He says, for example, the kingdom has come near.[14] The third paradox involves *signs of the coming of the kingdom* and Jesus tells His disciples that they can never determine the time of the coming because only the Father knows these things.[15] This last paradox looks to the horizon or furthest edge of history, what theologians call *eschatology*. However, it's apparent from the examples that this isn't just about what has traditionally been understood as 'last things'.

In the Lord's Prayer, Jesus teaches His disciples to pray 'Your kingdom come. Your will be done, on earth as in heaven.'[16] This is less about praying for the end of the age when the fullness of the Kingdom is revealed, and more about God's rule breaking into the here and now. So, it appears that the kingdom is not fixed in time and space, at least not in a sequential way that we understand.

Then there's another strand. The Gospels point to a mystical approach to the kingdom illustrated by Jesus telling His followers that the kingdom is within them[17] and to *enter the kingdom* is synonymous with becoming a disciple.[18] Clearly the Kingdom of God is not easy to define.

Donald Kraybill, in his book *The Upside-Down Kingdom* describes the kingdom like this:

'In broad strokes, most biblical scholars agree that the "Kingdom of God" means the dynamic rule or reign of God. The reign involves God's intentions, authority, and ruling power. It doesn't refer to a territory or a particular place. Nor is it static. It's dynamic- always becoming, spreading, and growing. The kingdom points us not to the place of God but to God's ruling activities. It is not a kingdom **in** *heaven, but* **from** *heaven – one that thrives here and now. The kingdom appears whenever women and men submit their lives to God's will.'* [19]

This may seem difficult to get our heads around but there is a model that helps us to think about the many faceted kingdom. To explore this further, we will dip our toes into the extraordinary world of quantum physics.

I was introduced to the quantum world by reading a book by Phil Mason called *Quantum Glory: The Science of Heaven Invading Earth.*[20] I am not a physicist and this book blew my mind. The author explores the intersection between the things that we read in the Bible and some of the most compelling discoveries in quantum physics. To weigh up these claims we must shrink the world down to the smallest of the small, below atoms to the sub-atomic level of the quantum realm. In quantum physics, we are observing what these minute packets of energy do and how they respond and interact with one another.

Experiments have shown that particles behave in certain ways that demonstrate that they cannot be localised in space and time, as in *our here and now*. This essentially means that they exist in another dimension other than ours. This kind of concept is standard fare for science fiction fans. Parallel worlds regularly feature in storylines and there are usually portals or gates between dimensions. Quantum physics, however, proposes that this is not fiction but an example of what is called *non-locality*. The phenomenon of "quantum tunnelling" illustrates the point. It demonstrates that "matter" has the capacity to de-materialise and then to re-materialise in the sub-atomic world. This is hard to grasp but when we put it alongside the story of Jesus just disappearing after revealing His identity on the Emmaus road, we might wonder if this is an example in action.[21] The non-local quantum world appears to be a kind of invisible, intermediate "buffer zone" between spirit and matter.[22] It's like a bridge between two dimensions or as Mason puts it, a veil between two worlds.

The concept of a veil between humanity and God and earth and heaven is one that we read in the Bible[23] but the dimensions that interact with one another are not only 'out there' in our surroundings.[24] Mason proposes that the spirit and soul of a human being is also a non-local buffer between the supernatural spirit of God and the physical body. This becomes the kingdom *within us*. It is then argued that when God heals someone who is physically sick, He does so via the invisible quantum world which instantaneously manifests in the world of matter.[25]

To put it more simply, the power of the Spirit from God's glory realm breaks through into our timeline and changes matter – *on earth as in heaven.* This restructures the physical world according to the will of God. Heaven essentially invades earth.

While we have been talking about paradox in relation to some features of the kingdom, it appears that the quantum world is full of such things. One of these is the *wave/particle duality*. Usually things are either waves (like sound) or particles (like dust), but then there is light - which is both wave and particle. Two mutually exclusive things that have always been understood to be *either/or* turn out to be *both-and*. The most extraordinary thing about this is that light can be both at the same time. Niels Bohr in 1926 called this *complementarity*, which means that something can be two different things at the same time.[26]

This brings us back to the difficulty of pinning the kingdom down to one thing, when it is clearly several - at the same time. God can be with His children all around the world simultaneously. This is not a problem if you are 'non-local' and not fixed by time or space to this earthly dimension. This invisible spiritual dimension that we call Heaven, according to what is revealed in the scriptures, is in constant engagement with the fixed material 'earthly' realm.

Throughout his book, Mason argues that these strange quantum phenomena may be able to shed light on some of the supernatural experiences in the Bible. He proposes that divine energy release from the *kingdom dimension* leads to the restructuring of matter, and the creation of new realities on a subatomic level, leading to healing and creative miracles in our dimension.

While Mason's book is fascinating, we have to recognise that not every quantum physicist shares these views, and many who engage with the mystical element of the quantum world gravitate toward an Eastern philosophy or New Age metaphysics. But Mason is not a lone voice. There are other well-respected scientists willing to go against the usual segregation of science and religion to explore this area from a different angle. One such scientist is John Polkinghorne, who was both a Professor of Mathematical Physics and a trained theologian. He wrote a book entitled *Quantum Physics and Theology : An Unexpected Kinship.*[27] In the introduction he writes:

> '..science and theology are both concerned with the

search for truth. In consequence, they complement each other rather than contrast one another. Of course the two disciplines focus on different dimensions of truth, but they share a common conviction that there is truth to be sought.' [28]

The subject of Quantum physics provides us with an interesting model for how the Kingdom of God may work in the interaction with our world. Whether this is an accurate picture is not really the point. What we know from the Bible is that Jesus demonstrates that the Kingdom of God can become visible in this world. We see it in the healings, deliverances, and resurrections. It makes possible what has been declared impossible, and the crowds are left with no rational explanation apart from it is the work of God. We also see it in the stories of people being transformed, not only in accounts in the Bible but throughout Christian history.

Like Christians around the world, I have prayed the Lord's prayer every day and in it I have said the words:

'Your kingdom come, Your will be done, on earth as in heaven.'

I am left wondering whether I've ever really understood the implications of this. It feels fundamental to my faith but I am at a loss to explain it. I know I won't add to my understanding unless I actively explore what the kingdom is about and what my role is in it. In his book, *When Heaven Invades Earth,* Bill Johnson writes:

'...*as disciples we are both citizens and ambassadors of another world. The world is our assignment, but not our home. Our purpose is eternal. The resources needed to complete the assignment are unlimited. The only restrictions are those between our ears.*' [29]

2

DETHRONING CAESAR

'The empire created the emperors - not the other way round'

Mary Beard

'The kingdom turns perceptions of power and hierarchy upside down, and with that inversion, comes an implied threat against the established order.'

The Ambassador

As I started to think more carefully about the subject of the kingdom, I considered what I understood the term to mean. The simple dictionary definition is of a country, state, or territory ruled by a king or queen.[1] However, can we talk about the Kingdom of God in the same way as we might talk about, for example, The United Kingdom? Or are earthly kingdoms and God's kingdom fundamentally different? I knew I needed to do some analysis at the start of this exploration so that I didn't end up importing my prior understanding of the term into what I was discovering about the Kingdom of God.

I began with the Bible and Roman history. I looked at the terms and concepts of the Roman world, and the language that the Apostle Paul uses in the New Testament. In the Roman understanding, the 'gospel' is the good news of Caesar having established peace and security. Caesar is the 'saviour' who has brought 'salvation' and therefore the people of the world should have 'faith' in their 'lord' – the emperor. This imperial language is borrowed by Paul, not to mimic it, but to subvert it.[2] Jesus is replacing Caesar, not as emperor but as the new Lord and Saviour who establishes peace. This comes not by military conquest, but by His self-giving on the cross. The symbol of His crucifixion then becomes a symbol of opposition to the empire and an inspiration for many to persist in their desire to sustain an alternative society.

This subversive re-purposing of terms is something that the Roman Empire couldn't ignore. Against a background of the imperial cult that decreed emperors were divine, if a growing number of oppressed people were to start proclaiming Jesus as Lord instead of Caesar,[3] then the authorities have a problem. This is one of the reasons why the early Christians were persecuted by Imperial Rome.

Jesus critiques the cultural hierarchies of His day by affirming kingdom values. When His disciples are arguing over who is the greatest in the kingdom of heaven, He answers their debate by placing a small child among them, saying:

'Truly I tell you, unless you change and become like little children, you will never enter the kingdom of heaven. Therefore, whoever takes the lowly position of this child is the greatest in the kingdom of heaven.' [4]

The kingdom turns perceptions of power and hierarchy upside down and, with that inversion comes an implied threat against the established order. The Biblical Scholar, Walter Wink, states:

'Not only did [Jesus] and his followers repudiate the autocratic values of power and wealth, but the institutions and systems that authorized and supported these values: the family, the Law, the sacrificial system, the Temple, kosher food regulations, the distinction between clean and unclean, patriarchy, role expectations for women and children, the class system, the use of violence, racial and ethnic divisions, the distinction between insider and outsider – indeed, every conceivable prop of domination, division and supremacy.' [5]

This re-definition of values demonstrates the kingdom's radical nature. It highlights the gulf between the Kingdom of God and worldly empires. When we study the history of the Christian Church, however, that gap is not always apparent. Though we may believe that the Church should reflect kingdom values, in practice it often drifts away from its radical core, making it indistinguishable from the empires around it. It costs to stand against the prevailing powers and sometimes compromise seems preferable to conflict. I suspect that most of us know what that feels like.

My exploration into the differences between kingdom and empire received an unexpected push one morning, when I received a prompt from God. I woke up with a phrase running through my head about 'dethroning Caesar'. I have never used this phrase before, nor do I remember reading it anywhere. I wondered whether God was encouraging me to explore areas where I had compromised, embracing a model that was more about empire than kingdom. To take this further, I began to study the power of empire and see where my understanding, values, or practices lined up with it.

Professor Mary Beard's quotation that empire creates emperors rather than the other way round, illuminated an important point. Empire is the container that shapes, forms, and defines community life and culture. It's not just about its physical manifestations, such as its buildings, systems, and institutions. It's also about an inner spiritual reality involving corporate vision, culture, and collective personality. This means that its sum is greater than its parts.

In the New Testament, this perspective is bound up with what the Bible calls *Principalities and Powers*.[6] Walter Wink has written extensively about these. He argues that the term relates to the spirituality at the centre of political, economic, and cultural institutions of the day. It isn't just a personification, it is a real aspect of the institution; a spiritual ethos, whether recognised as one or not.[7]

Wink veers away from using the language of demons and angels, but he is still speaking about a spiritual and invisible dimension which is indirectly perceptible by means of projection. An institution's 'spirit' is felt or recognised in some way. He uses the expression *the domination system* to indicate what happens when an entire network of Powers becomes integrated around idolatrous values.[8]

Rome in the first century C.E. illustrates this system well, but it is not just Superpowers that operate in this way. Every institution has a spirituality which, when part of the domination system, will resist transformation. Change will not come with a replacement of personnel at the top if the system behind it is left intact because its 'spirit,' or core values, will still operate and control. If the system does not change, then the new leaders will be created in line with the existing cultural mores. When this happens, it's likely that, despite hopeful beginnings, optimism will evaporate further down the road when nothing has truly altered. We see this common pattern in organisations, in governments, and even in churches.

Although I was beginning to understand the connections between the domination system and empire, I was still unclear about all the inferences of 'dethroning Caesar' in my life. The term implies that it is not God who is on the throne but an agent of empire, which amounts to idolatry. I asked myself when had I listened more to the voice of empire rather than to God? I didn't remember a specific time, but that is the point. Empire's values go with the flow of the world's cultures. We do not usually challenge them because they feel normal. It is only when we embrace kingdom values that a light goes on, illuminating the difference. This sets up a conflict of interests and the empire certainly likes to strike back.

Coercive control is a standard tool of the domination system and, through manipulation, it draws us into colluding with half-truths which, of course, are still deceits. Take, for example, the virtue of humility. Being humble is valued throughout the Bible[9] as a worthy trait. Jesus teaches that anyone who wants to be first must be the very last and the servant of all.[10] However, when humility becomes compulsive or un-reflective, it can morph into self-abasement. This is a distortion of this beautiful virtue. It also makes people vulnerable to being controlled by others.

Under the righteous banner of humility, the domination system prospers, urging us to stay small and insignificant, not to over-reach ourselves or shine too brightly next to others. In the guise of virtue, we are kept in a rigid hierarchy, accepting the way of the world and our place in it, constantly deferring to those 'above' us and not speaking out. If we are not sure whether we are part of a domination system, a good test is to start asking difficult questions and see what response we receive. As a woman, I have encountered the attitude - sometimes openly, but more often, covertly: *nobody likes a mouthy woman who doesn't know her place in the scheme of things.*

But that's empire, not kingdom.

In organisational terms, Jesus did appoint leaders and, out of them, He had an inner circle of Peter, James, and John, but this tier of leadership was not rigidly hierarchical. He gave responsibility to others to go out and share the good news of the kingdom, first to the twelve disciples, and then, to the seventy-two. In Luke 9 and 10, we read that both groups have the same instructions, delegated authority, and opportunities. No one is considered too lowly in the pecking order to carry kingdom power.

Perhaps the most poignant image that we have of

Jesus subverting hierarchy is in John 13, when Jesus takes the role of a servant and washes the disciples' feet. Leadership takes on a different nature in the kingdom, and this clashes with the domination system common in empire.

One of the ways that we challenge the domination system is to question its legitimacy. Being the voice in the wilderness is threatening to a regime that requires persuasive ideology and propaganda to hold it up. John the Baptist knew that when he ended up in Herod's dungeon, and it is no surprise that the Apostle John was exiled by the Powers to the island of Patmos where he had his visions, recorded in the book of Revelation. As Wink says:

'A seer whose vision cuts through the atmospherics of imperial legitimation is a far worse threat than armed revolutionaries who accept the ideology of domination and merely desire it for themselves.' [11]

What this means is that we can claim back our power from the system, and de-legitimatise that same system in the process. We can walk in the freedom that Jesus has won for us through the cross, but it requires us to renounce the agreement we have made with deception and to cut that tie with the domination system itself. We can do this through the practice of repentance. This is about changing our minds. It's turning around and going a different way, so we're in the right position to go forward. Tom Wright summarises it like this:

'If the enslaving powers are to be overthrown, they must be robbed of their power base; and their power base is...that humans hand over power to them by worshipping them instead of worshipping the Creator, by the idolatry and consequent distortion of life that can be lumped together as "sin." Once that sin has been dealt with, the power of the idols is broken; once the Messiah has been "made sin for us," the way is open for the ministry of reconciliation to fan out in all directions.' [12]

Wright argues that sin is a human failure of vocation. We are 'image-bearers' and are made to reign in life[13] which is why we are 'kingdom-people' not subjects of the empire. When we turn away from this truth, we relinquish our rights and end up being enslaved. Wright describes the problem from God's side when he says:

'When God looks at sin, what he sees is what a violin maker would see if the player were to use his lovely creation as a tennis racquet.' [14]

As image-bearers, we are who God says we are, not what empire tries to make us believe so that we can be coerced and controlled. Worship helps to re-order our perceptions and put God back on the throne. When this happens, everything else comes into alignment. It opens channels of communication and helps us to recognise both our inheritance and our responsibility as children of God. When we turn away from where we have been and move into our proper position and role, His power flows through us and all distorted images that have been holding sway over us crumble.

After this period of reflection, which was rewarding but hard work, I was longing for some lightness in my spirit. Where better to find joy and relaxation than The Beach? So I settled down to connect with the Secret Place to engage with Abba, Jesus and Rhema again.

3

UNION

"Help us to find God"
"No one can help you there."
"Why not?'
"For the same reason that no one can help the fish to find the ocean."

Anthony de Mello

'We become what we are called to be if we are willing to believe God, let Him forge our identity, and draw us into our destiny.'

The Ambassador

In the Epilogue of *The Beach*, I entered a dark place but was still able to hear the sound of the sea within me. It reminded me that, wherever I was, there was still part of me on The Beach. After a lot of mental processing about dethroning Caesar, I longed to go back to rest and enjoy God's presence in the Secret Place.

As I sat quietly, I dedicated my imagination to God and went through its gate to find the Holy Three, leaving behind any anxiety or heaviness. Before long, I could feel the warmth on my face, the wind in my hair and I heard the waves. I was instantly calm and relaxed and I felt the tension in my body dissolve. Then I stepped into the water and walked along the shore. My heart leapt when I saw Abba, Jesus, and Rhema, and I knew that their love was all I needed.

I was beginning to enjoy the sense of freedom. Nothing else mattered in that moment than just being there with Them. My heart was filled with joy and I felt full of light. I was instantly made welcome. They were so pleased to see me. It shone from their faces as they smiled at me and we laughed together.

I felt like crying – it was a homecoming. Like little children, we made a circle with our arms holding onto each other, laughing, and going around and around in circles in the water. There was no point to it; it was the giddy exuberance of being with the people you love.

After a while we fell into the shallow water and

laughed, just looking at one another. Everything else fell away. I didn't know if anyone spoke these words verbally or not, and, if so, who it was, but this was the chorus of their heart for me.

'Mandy, you are always with us; it's just sometimes you don't remember that. Your heart can be filled with love and joy on The Beach whenever you want it to be. You're here always but you're also in your other dimension day by day. You don't have to climb to glory because you're here with us anyway. We are one – but you sometimes still go looking for us because 'you' in yourself are elsewhere. Your mind takes many twists and turns, but your heart is rooted with us on The Beach. It just takes a bit of time for your mind to catch up to where your heart already is.

Living in two locations is normal. You are here with us now and this is as real as anything. Just because it's happening in your Spirit doesn't make it less real. Your body is rooted where you live day to day, but it's affected by where you are in the Spirit too.

This is part of what being an ambassador is. You start to connect with those two locations building a bigger, wider bridge between the two. An ambassador is not just a representative of their birth country living elsewhere. They need to go back and forth, bringing communications and resources from their homeland. They are a conduit; a channel of power. They do not have authority by themselves. This comes from who they represent. It is delegated from the ruler of their home country, where they have their citizenship.

We have taken you through dethroning Caesar as we want your capacity to carry our love, power, and grace to increase, but we couldn't do that without freeing up more space within you. This meant taking power away from the idols and the things that restrict you. We couldn't force this on you as that would violate love. You have free will and so we lead you into understanding and leave the rest to you. When you renounce these ties, repent, and ask for forgiveness, you kick out the pretenders and free up more space within to carry Our love message to the world. Well done for taking that step. We're so pleased you made that decision.

When you can carry greater capacity in yourself, We can work together more. You come to represent Us more in your everyday life. It is the process of creating new wineskins for the new wine [1] *that is flowing even now. Relinquishing control, releasing old patterns that have kept you bound and restricted by legalism and the agreements you have made, frees you up. Don't worry that it's not done. When you have said the Powers have to go and withdrawn your consent for them to operate, they have to comply. They will lie and pretend they are in charge, tying you up in knots and getting you to question your freedom. Do not be fooled. If you have removed their legal rights, they have to go and Our presence shoos them away.*

More of your heart operates on kingdom values and holds Our grace. Receive Our love and let it flow into all those corners of your heart that are parched and cracked. Let Us water the thirsty ground and let it bloom. Practice coming back to Us frequently, enjoying Our time together, receiving from Us. Let that bridge become well-travelled and take back with you everything you need to water the earth and make the desert bloom. What We do in you, you will share with others and they will flourish. We will never leave you and you will never leave Us if you don't want to.'

I HAD ALREADY DISCOVERED in *The Beach* that God is in the *process* of things. God takes us step by step towards the purpose He has called us to. He makes big promises that most of us would feel anxious about or unprepared for, but He also says He will never leave us. These are important factors to hold onto when we are thinking about what it means to be an ambassador.

I love the fact that Moses spends the majority of two chapters in the book of Exodus arguing with God, finding all the reasons why he shouldn't be the one to go to Pharaoh and demand freedom for his people. Another unlikely hero in the Hebrew Scriptures is Gideon. He receives his commission when he is in a winepress, threshing wheat to keep it from the Midianites who are oppressing the Israelites, ruining their crops, and invading the land. An angel appears and says that the Lord is with him and calls Gideon a 'mighty warrior.'[2] He is being sent to save Israel out of Midian's hand. The irony of this great deliverer hiding out in a winepress is not lost on Gideon and, like Moses before him, he starts to argue with God along the lines of 'you don't mean me'. He says:

'Pardon me, my lord...but how can I save Israel? My clan is the weakest in Manasseh and I am the least in my family.' [3]

Again, the message is that God will be with him, which is not what Gideon wants to hear when he doesn't feel up to the task. Later in the story, Gideon still wants assurance that God will save Israel by his hand, so he places a wool fleece on the threshing floor and bargains that if in the morning, there is dew on the fleece but the ground is dry, then he will take this as a confirmation that what he's heard is true. The next morning he has his answer when he wrings out the dew from the sodden fleece on the dry ground. However, this still isn't enough, and he asks for another test. For the next morning he asks for the opposite: a dry fleece on a ground covered with dew. God graciously and patiently gives him his confirmation.

It is encouraging that these big names in scripture had many of the anxieties and failings that we do. Their identity and calling came solely through God, not from their own belief about themselves or how they were seen by their community. It is the same for us. We don't earn or deserve what God gives us; we receive it as a gift of grace. God doesn't desert us after He's commissioned us either. He gives us strength and teaches us, and there is usually plenty to learn along the way. Instant transformation is less common than the more dogged procedure of learning, practice, and persisting through our circumstances. We become what we are called to be if we are willing to believe God, let Him forge our identity, and draw us into our destiny.

These reflections helped me to realise that the weighty call to be an ambassador and represent the Kingdom is not a problem for a God who is committed to our development and progression. In fact, we have the assurance that God who begins a good work in us will carry it on to completion.[4]

This process requires us to remember that God is with us. He hasn't just set things in motion and then gone off for an extended tea break. He is present with us continually. This is not a new concept. Every Christmas I preach about the Incarnation. It is the time to focus on the promise of God revealed in the scriptures:

'The virgin will conceive and give birth to a son, and they will call him Immanuel (which means 'God with us').' [5]

Sam Wells has written extensively about the phrase *'God with us'*. [6] He states:

'God's whole being is shaped to be with. Being with is about presence, about participation, about partnership.' [7]

We see this first in the nature of the Trinity, where God is three persons in one substance. They are with one another in perfect unity, and yet still diverse and distinct as persons. When we talk about the Incarnation, we are referring to God the Son taking on human form to live among us in the person of Jesus Christ. It is God's commitment to be *with* us. This is not an exclusive choice with losers and outsiders, it is what Wells calls:

'an inclusive covenant, held with fierce intensity, as if each one were the only one.' [8]

We therefore see these two dynamics at work. God's perfect inner relationship (within the Trinity itself) and God's very life shaped to be in relation-ship with us through Jesus in the power of the Holy Spirit.[9] We are invited to share in the life of the Trinity and Jesus refers to this union in John 15, when He tells His disciples that He is the true vine and we are the branches. He instructs them to:

'Remain in me, as I also remain in you. No branch can bear fruit by itself; it must remain in the vine. Neither can you bear fruit unless you remain in me.' [10]

One of the major themes in the prayer that Jesus prays before He is arrested is unity. It is about the oneness of Jesus with the Father, and a prayer for the disciples to be one also. He prays to Abba saying:

'I have given them the glory that you gave me, that they may be one as we are one – I in them and you in me – so that we may be brought to complete unity.' [11]

This is Jesus' prayer for all His followers, but apart from a high point in Acts 4: 32-35 where it says, *'all the believers were one in heart and mind,'* this kind of unity has often proved elusive, or difficult to sustain, throughout the Church's history. Perhaps one of the reasons for this is that 'being with' is not very easy. Often we find 'doing for' more comfortable. Sam Wells challenges us all by asking:

'Does my doing for arise out of a fundamental commitment to be with, or is my doing for driven by my profound desire to avoid the discomfort, the challenge, the patience, the loss of control involved in being with?' [12]

Reflecting on this challenge, I can see that there is an uncomfortable difference between doing *for* and being *with*. However well-meaning or altruistic an action is, when it is done for rather than with, it is more paternalistic in nature. I recognise this in a project that our church gets involved with at Christmas. We join with another parish in an urban area where there are much higher levels of deprivation and we put together and deliver hampers to local vulnerable families. It is a positive and loving action that brings material gifts to those who are struggling at Christmas and we receive so much back from participating in it. However excellent the project is, and I still believe that it is thoroughly worthwhile, it remains a 'for', rather than a 'with', project. Mother Theresa draws attention to the crux of the matter when she writes:

'Today it is very fashionable to talk about the poor. Unfortunately, it is not fashionable to talk with them.' [13]

Heidi Baker, co-founder of the missionary organisation, Iris Global, has lived and worked with poor communities around the world. She writes:

'When God sent me to the poor, it was not for what I could give, but for what I could learn and for what I could receive. God did not start by telling me to minister to the poor but to be ministered to by them. We need to start talking with them...I asked God to help me understand the poor. He told me to go sit with the children. I reminded God that I had a PhD in systematic theology, and I said, "I don't do children." He told me, "You do children now." [14]

Heidi and Rolland Baker's inspiring stories exemplify what it really means to be *with* others, but it requires humility and a willingness to come out of our comfort zone. This is not just about how we relate to other people; this is the key to greater intimacy with God. Love, peace, and joy are an essential part of this, but it also involves plenty of challenge.

We see in the Gospels that Jesus is not easy to be with all the time. As the embodiment of God's fierce and utter holiness,[15] He brings light and truth to every situation and that revelation can be hard to bear. Although He never fails to be with each person he meets, some cannot be with Him.[16] We have examples of this in the Gospels when people turn away from following Him, make excuses, or become angry at His words.[17] Our own spiritual journey involves an ever-increasing experience of living in His love, light and truth and letting that transform us from within. It is a process of being *with* that makes the difference, whereas doing *for* may leave many areas of our lives untouched.

Being consciously aware of the presence of Jesus in the present tense of our lives changes the dynamic of our faith. Rather than an historical figure in the Bible, where we might say "Jesus *was*...", we speak in terms of "Jesus *is*..." In the usual conundrum that theology throws up, time is not a linear, measurable, quantity when it comes to God, because Jesus was, is, and ever shall be. When we look at the scriptures, the truth about Jesus is not just located in, and confined to, a specific historical time and geographical context, it is applied for all time. This means that when we look, for example, at what the Apostle Paul writes about in the New Testament about our unity in Jesus, he isn't just talking to the missional communities in his context; he's talking to us too. When we think of union with God, we return to scripture to see how it applies to us.

Paul uses the words *in-Christ* many times in his

letters to illustrate how faith in Jesus connects us to His story, and how we share the benefits of all that He has achieved through the cross. Writing to the believers in Rome, Paul says that we who are baptised into Christ Jesus have been baptised into His death. We were crucified with Christ, and buried with Him, so that when Christ was raised from the dead, we too may live a new life.[18] The sacrament of baptism focuses on this *death-to-new-life* journey in the words of the service and its symbolism. We become one with Jesus as He is one with us. This is not just a nice tradition, a bit of church ritual with a party afterwards; this is union with Christ. While I am not criticising the 'sprinkling' that goes on in our church fonts, the visual example of a full-immersion baptism can conjure up more powerfully what this sacrament is about.

Alongside this identification with Christ for salvation, Ephesians 2: 4-6 says:

'But because of his great love for us, God, who is rich in mercy, made us alive with Christ even when we were dead in transgressions – it is by grace you have been saved. And God raised us up with Christ and seated us with him in the heavenly realms in Christ Jesus'

It is the easiest thing in the world to say that all this unity language is purely symbolic; these passages are just theological attempts to explain the new life we have in Jesus and to indicate our union with Him. But what if they are not? What if there is a sense in which we really are in two places at once?

There are stories of mystics, such as the nineteenth century Franciscan Priest, Padre Pio, who was known to bi-locate, but this is not what I'm talking about. I'm referring to every follower of Jesus having part of them seated in heavenly places because of our union with Him. To consider this further I find myself, once again, reaching for illustrations from the quantum physics field as an example of what this might be like. Phil Mason states:

'It is a unique property of the quantum world that sub-atomic particles have the capacity to be in two places at the same time...In our macroscopic world of classical physics the last thing we would expect is to see someone bilocate right before our eyes so that suddenly they can be in two places at the same time. Yet, in the counter-intuitive world of the quantum universe this is exactly what is going on all the time. Electrons have the ability to be in two places at once. [19]

So much of what we are learning about the quantum world challenges our understanding of time, space, energy, and matter. If we take some of the phenomena that have been consistently demonstrated by experiments in quantum mechanics and apply them to what we read in the Bible, there are some startling connections. Electrons being in two places at once is just one of them.

If, the kingdom is *within* us,[20] then it makes

sense that there may be a 'buffer-zone' or 'veil' between us and the realm of God - all in the one human, tripartite body. God can import anything from the kingdom straight into our spirits. One might argue that much of the journey of faith is about the process of becoming aware or what God is already doing. It is not unlike the quotation from the start of this chapter where no one can help fish to find the ocean; they are already immersed in it and swimming around in it. They only need the revelation that they already have everything they have been looking for. If God is with us and within us, then the only barrier is our awareness of that truth. The Psalmist describes it in lyrical terms:

> *'Where can I go from your Spirit?*
> *Where can I flee from your presence?*
> *If I go up to the heavens, you are there;*
> *If I make my bed in the depths, you are there.*
> *If I rise on the wings of the dawn,*
> *If I settle on the far side of the sea,*
> *Even there your hand will guide me,*
> *Your right hand will hold me fast.*
> *If I say, 'Surely the darkness will hide me and the*
> *light become night around me,*
> *even the darkness will not be dark to you;*
> *the night will shine like the day,*
> *for darkness is as light to you.'* [21]

Another way of thinking about this is to use a technological image. In our kitchen, we have a speaker that can play music from a phone via a Blue-tooth connection. The phone needs to be 'paired' first with the speaker to forge a connection, then the music can be transmitted from the phone and heard through the speakers. We are like those speakers, picking up on the frequency of what is transmitting. If our receiver is 'paired' with God's transmitter, then a connection is made that means we can receive and then transmit God's heart. However, there can be a battle over what is received. When several of the family are travelling in the car, the Bluetooth music system doesn't always connect to the phone we want. It might connect to another device and then we must repeat the pairing process so that the right sound is made.

Although all images tend to break down if we push them too far, it can be helpful to think of us as having that pairing facility within us and that it is primed to connect with God. We still have a choice, however, in what we listen to and what we play through the 'speakers' of our life. Many close it down and God allows for that in His provision of free will. However, if we decide to open that connec-tion in pairing with God, then why can we not be seated in heavenly realms as well as located here in this time and space? If we are in union with God in our spirit, it means that we can exist in two dimen-sions at the same time. We have heard all these storylines in science-fiction, but what if what we're learning from quantum mechanics is taking this concept into science-fact?

It's good to keep our minds open to possibilities as we journey into what it means to be an ambassador. It just might help us to step up to the role with greater assurance that our king and the kingdom is much closer than we may think.

4
————

RELAPSE

"Y ou don't have to see the whole staircase, just take the first step."

Martin Luther King

'Was I trying to push ahead on my own, instead of relaxing into a partnership with Jesus? Was I attempting to run before I could walk? And did God have some things that He needed to deal with in me before I could see the breakthrough I longed for? I felt the answer to all those questions was 'yes'.

The Ambassador

In 2021, I went to see the neurologist again and was told that the migraines I suffered were not frequent enough to qualify for the new treatment of preventative injections. Migraine is very common in the population and the new methods of combatting it are extremely expensive. It made sense that those whose lives were most adversely affected would get access to these, ahead of the rest of us. However, as a chronic sufferer of thirty-three years, I was disappointed when the advice from the neurologist was solely to increase the dose of medication I had tried before - with little success. The consoling news was that this visit coincided with the period of experiences I had with the Trinity on The Beach.

I had been encouraged by Abba to look at my choices and how fear infected my thoughts and general well-being. I researched how the body and mind processed trauma and learned about the fear, flight, and freeze responses. Through my reading, I was also introduced to the concept of neuroplastic pain and the fear-pain cycle. What I noticed most was that taking a holistic view under the direction of The Trinity was having health benefits. Over the year, the migraines were becoming less severe, even though I was still experiencing one or two forty-eight hour episodes in a month. Being able to carry on with life to a large degree, without being forced to retreat to a darkened room with a bowl to be sick in, was a victory of sorts.

Whenever I had the first twinge of pain and thought I was getting 'one of those', I would consciously try to relax, letting go of tension and being more mindful about what I was doing. I had a nasal spray to take at its onset, but I found that, though this stopped the migraine, it returned the next day, and I was tired and rather 'spaced' from taking the medication. Over time, and with improvement of my symptoms, I let it run its course without reaching for a nasal spray.

It was the Summer of 2022 when I had a relapse. It wasn't a 'full-blown, super-vomiting, looking-like-death' relapse, but it was bad enough. It was probably because I was doing what the neuroplastic pain researchers told me not to: I was putting myself under pressure to get rid of it. Alan Gordon, one of the experts in this field of treating neuroplastic pain, writes about three predictable stages that patients go through when they relapse. The first is panic. Patients who have been managing their pain are suddenly shocked by having a relapse. They then try to overcome their panic by doing all the right things, but this is often with the wrong mindset. He states:

'Instead of self-compassion and lightness, they're doing it with an undercurrent of desperation and pressure.' [1]

This signals the second stage of relapse which Gordon describes as 'forcing it.' It is only when the patient can turn down the intensity while being outcome independent, that the third stage arrives, which is when the relapse goes away.

Gordon warns patients that there is no automatic

pass to stage three of the relapse process, because it's difficult not to panic when the pain hits, and it's impossible not to feel desperate in stage two. It takes time to get past the shock. Knowing the process, however, gives the patient power and builds resilience. We know what to expect when it happens and how to move through our body's responses, knowing our symptoms will resolve themselves. Gordon states:

'The key to staying out of pain is the same as the key to getting out of pain; you want to make your brain feel safe.' [2]

I recognised I had been trying to force it. If I prayed harder, or perhaps commanded or decreed God's Word louder, maybe it would go, and I would be free from migraines for life. It was an attractive prospect that, paradoxically, encouraged me down the very route that sparked a relapse.

The reason I had engaged more forcefully with my symptoms was due to my developing theology. I had gone in search of the kingdom and discovered it was within me due to the union I have with Jesus through faith. Therefore, I believed that I should be able to access the realm of God's rule and all its treasures, which includes divine healing. I believed that God was encouraging me to seek the kingdom[3] and had given it to me because He is a good Father[4] who knows how to give good things to His children[5]. I wanted to prove to myself that these are more than fine-sounding concepts but to do this, I would need to demonstrate the practical outworking of this truth in my life. Theoretical theology isn't much use if I don't experience the benefits myself.

Pete Carter, in his book *Unwrapping Lazarus,* speaks about the gap between our input and our output calling it *spiritual malabsorption.* He writes:

'Spiritual malabsorption is a common malady. So much input, so little growth. How many sermons have I listened to, how many chapters of the Bible read and re-read? So much head knowledge. Even when we have grown in faith in the past, has that growth been sustained?' [6]

This was an uncomfortable question. I recognised that my reality fell short of my expectations. It just didn't work. Or at least, it didn't work in the way I thought it should. Perhaps I was being naïve, and it wasn't as simple as that. Yet when I think about the male disciples being called 'ordinary, unschooled men,'[7] I am sure that they didn't have to tie themselves up in mental knots so they could see a miracle among them.

When the migraine was gone, I was left reflecting on why I had the relapse. Was I trying to push ahead on my own, instead of relaxing into a partnership with Jesus? Was I attempting to run before I could walk? And did God have some things that He needed to deal with *in me* before I could see the breakthrough I longed for? I felt the answer to all those questions was 'yes'.

I concluded that, to behave as an ambassador I must become more in tune with the One who sends me. I am not representing myself, but the king of the kingdom. Although He is my focus, I still have a responsibility. I am to make room for Him, and I do this by ditching the things that perpetually get in the way. As the writer of the letter to the Hebrews says:

'Therefore, since we are surrounded by such a great cloud of witnesses, let us throw off everything that hinders and the sin that so easily entangles. And let us run with perseverance the race marked out for us, fixing our eyes on Jesus, the pioneer and perfecter of faith.' [8]

There was plenty that entangled me and weighed me down and, every time I dealt with some of it, another thing reared its head, making me wonder whether I was making any progress at all. I recalled my husband's face when I shared with him my latest trials. He smiled affectionately at me and said: "*It must be so tiring being you.*" I laughed because he was right.

5

PARTNERS IN BORROWED SHOES

'*The shoes He made for you will not fit anyone else. Fill them.*'

Heidi Baker

'*Our authentic selves are desperate to see the light of day and to breathe easily and deeply into our lives, but so often we are stuffing them down, silencing them, and making them less than God has made them to be.*'

The Ambassador

Frustrating and disappointing as my relapse was, God still showed His goodness to me through it. When I eventually fell asleep, I had an interesting dream. It wasn't like those I had about The Beach: it involved an image of some prophetic art I'd been given years earlier.

Some years ago, I was given a picture by a friend who said that God had told her to give it to me. She didn't know why, but she was obedient and passed it onto me. In the picture there is a small, blonde-haired child in a pair of jeans and a blue shirt bending down with her hands in a pool of water. The reflection in the water is not the child but a mighty lion. What my friend didn't realise was that the child looked extremely like I had at that age, even down to the hairstyle and the jeans. (I was never a girl who loved her dresses.) Growing up next door to farmland and not having computers or smartphones to distract me, I had played outside. Most children did. It might be in their street, in their garden if they had one, or further afield. Children roamed more freely than they do now, probably because there wasn't the same level of knowledge and anxiety about predators. In my case, I remember climbing trees, going pond dipping, and exploring the local environment. Not only did the child in the picture look like me, but she was playing in the countryside as I had done.

Looking at the reflection in the water and having read C. S. Lewis' book *The Lion, The Witch and The Wardrobe,* I was reminded of Aslan, the lion in the story. Aslan represents Jesus and therefore this piece of art was saying something very powerful about our connection with Christ and our identity in Him. I have always liked the picture and I had stuck it on my office door, but I didn't know why it was that image that was being brought to my mind.

After posting the picture on my social media, I asked my friends to help me find the artist. One of them told me it was by the fine artist, Marilyn Simandle. I found the painting on her website under the section for Prophetic Art. It is called 'Partners'. The artist writes:

'This print tells of who we are and whose we are. Our identity is in the Lion of Judah. We are what we are from the inside out. As we collaborate with Jesus we get to bring heaven to earth. As we lose ourselves in this print we begin to truly believe who we are' [1]

This took me back to the prophetic word from December 2021 which I've recounted in the prologue of this book. God had told me *'you're going to live inside-out'* and bringing heaven to earth was all about the kingdom being made visible in this dimension. It was an encouragement to keep going and to keep being a partner with Jesus. It also reminded me that I am best at doing that when I have that child-like faith that Jesus talked about in the Gospels.[2]

While I recognise the wisdom of accepting both our light and shade, I also know that life can feel lighter and freer when we get rid of some of our junk. The spiritual writer, Paulo Coelho, puts it beautifully when he says:

'*Maybe the journey isn't so much about becoming anything. Maybe it's about un-becoming everything that isn't really you so you can be who you were meant to be in the first place.*'

This resonated with me. My experiences on The Beach had drawn me into a season of seeing where fear affected my life, and now I felt another period of discernment was required, to 'un-become' the things I had taken on which didn't belong to me.

We all have areas of our lives where we have seen ourselves through others' eyes and accepted their vision as truth. Or perhaps we have compromised ourselves to fit in to avoid the challenge of being different or even being seen at all. We can contort ourselves into a mould that was never meant for us and then we wonder why we are so uncomfortable. Our authentic selves are desperate to see the light of day and to breathe easily and deeply into our lives, but so often we are stuffing them down, silencing them, and making them less than God has made them to be. Heidi Baker writes:

'*God has a special pair of shoes just for you, perfectly suited for your own path. You must learn to wear your own shoes and never put on anyone else's. Walk in your anointing.*' [3]

Meeting the challenge to walk in our own shoes requires us to decide what belongs to us and what doesn't. It involves a process of reflection and the courage to make decisions for ourselves. When we are young, it is normal that we wear the shoes that are provided by our family. At that age, we don't have another choice. However, some of us are *still* wearing these same shoes and we haven't swapped them for ones we've chosen ourselves. Or perhaps we are choosing to wear a style to please someone else. We are taught from a young age how we fit into the world and how we ensure that we remain acceptable. At times, this learning works against us for the sake of keeping the status quo and fulfilling what the dominant culture desires. It can lead to many destructive and self-negating things masquerading as the truth.

As we assert our own choices and live from our authentic selves we may find that we run into conflict with others. We are not fitting in with them in the way we're expected to. They may even take our desire to choose our own shoes as a rejection of *them*. However, standing in our own shoes is essential if we are to become the people God calls us to be. This is not just about looking to the future, this is also about dealing with the past. As I was discovering in this process of formation, God often takes us on a journey to let go of those things that weigh us down. This is more difficult to do when we are still wearing someone else's shoes because we are not properly owning our feelings.

Forgiveness is an important part of letting go and the Therapist, Melody Beattie, advocates forgiving *after* we feel our feelings not before. If we don't own our feelings we live with the denial of them. This prevents them being processed and healed. She writes:

'Sadly, many of us have had no place to go with all that anger. We swallow it, bite our tongues, stiffen our shoulders, push it into our stomachs, let it rattle around in our heads, run from it, medicate it, or give it a cookie. We blame ourselves, turn anger into depression, put ourselves to bed, hope to die, and get sick because of it. Finally we ask God to forgive us for being such horrible people for feeling anger in the first place.' [4]

It is therefore no surprise that when we rush to forgive without first 'feeling our feelings' we don't feel lighter by the end of it and the pain persists. Beattie states:

'Forgiving and forgetting feed our denial system. We need to think about, remember, understand, and make good decisions about what we are forgiving, what can be forgotten, and what is still a problem. And forgiving someone does not mean we have to let that person keep hurting us.' [5]

When we take the borrowed shoes off our feet, we can feel the freedom to stretch, and be more fully our authentic selves. There's always work still to be done but finding our own shoes and putting them on is an important part of the formation process for all of us.

6

UNFINISHED BUSINESS

'*Most Christians have repented enough to be forgiven, but not enough to see the kingdom. They go part of the way, then stop.*'

Bill Johnson

'*God is committed to our development, and that involves both growth and letting go.*'

The Ambassador

I was mulling over the attributes of an ambassador and finding that there seemed to be a lot of formation involved. Although using 'process' appeared to be God's preferred way of doing things, as I reached my fifty-second birthday, I couldn't help feeling that God could get on with it now. I was focused on *chronos* time: the sequential passing of days, weeks, months, and years, but God, being outside of time, seemed to work on a *kairos* schedule instead. This is the point when everything comes into perfect alignment and His purposes are fulfilled. Although I bowed to His superior vision and planning, it didn't prevent me from being grumpy.

In the case of being an ambassador, I grudgingly admitted that preparation was necessary. Like the prophetic art painting described in the previous chapter, God and I were partners. He would help me to get ready for the next stage by ridding me of what was getting in the way of my growth and flourishing. Jesus talks about this in John 15, where He is the vine and His Father is the gardener. He says that the Father,

'cuts off every branch in me that bears no fruit, while every branch that does bear fruit he prunes so that it will be even more fruitful.' [1]

The pastor and writer, Kris Vallotton, takes this image and explains the consequences if this is not done. He says:

'If you don't prune the branch all the way back to its fruitfulness, then the vine's capacity to produce fruit will be siphoned off to grow sticks.' [2]

In our partnership, God wanted to ensure that I was able to carry what He was going to give me, without it damaging or destroying me. He didn't want me to burst like an old wineskin when new wine is poured into it, or to tear like an old garment, because a patch of unshrunk cloth is sown onto it.[3] My frustration in this matter was not solely due to my impatience, but because it was an uncomfortable experience. The Methodist Chaplain from my university days always said: *"There is no growth without pain"* and I have found this to be true.

The process of refining people is like refining metal. When gold is purified, the container is placed in the fire until the impurities come to the surface as it melts. These are then carefully skimmed off. The Refiner knows when the metal is completely pure because they can look at the surface and, like a mirror, it will reflect their face. Bill Johnson writes:

'It is this same process by which Jesus refines us. He does so until He can see His likeness is us. That is the real reason for refinement – to reveal Jesus on earth.' [4]

It would make sense therefore that, to represent Jesus as an ambassador, some refining is required. Facing increased heat and letting the impurities become visible is all part of the process. Such suffering and perseverance may produce character,[5] but that is easy to forget when we are in the miserable thick of it.

The images of cleaning, pruning, refining, stretching, releasing, growing, and developing are woven all the way through the Bible. Faith is not a static experience. We must be ready to welcome His fire to burn up the dross within or to embrace the wind of the Spirit to blow away the chaff, leaving only what is fruitful. God is committed to our development, and that involves both growth and letting go.

I had already made a start on this by increasing my awareness of what didn't belong to my authentic self. I also recognised that there were unhealed parts of me that sometimes got in the way of my best intentions. Opening myself up to the healing of God required a journey of radical repentance, but I embarked on it in the knowledge that I was welcome, and unconditionally loved by God, not accused and rejected for my short-comings.

Repentance is a religious word. In the Church, it is a formal part of our liturgy in our prayers of penitence. We may have a moment of quiet as we think about those things where we have missed God's best for us and then we say the words of *Confession* together. It's a public declaration that we are sorry and want to turn around to that newness of life that God offers, knowing that when we realign with God's truth, He will forgive us and wipe the slate clean. As a priest, I usually stand up at this part of the service and declare the words of *Absolution* over us all. This is to pronounce God's forgiveness for sin. It's easy to think '*Right. Job done. All sorted. Now let's get on with the rest of the worship service.*' But I sometimes wonder whether this brief interlude ever really connects us with the reality of falling short of God's standard for us[6]. We may call to mind a recent example of where we missed the mark, but do we really connect with its impact on God, on others, or ourselves? I am not proposing that we wear sack cloth and ashes and lament with self-flagellation, but I wonder if our repentance just doesn't go far enough.

This is not about penance. The New Testament writers argue that Jesus has already set us free from sin through His death on the cross.[7] This is about renewing our minds and changing our direction so we can live from God's perspective. When this is our goal, significant reflection is required. Some of us find it helpful to work through our issues with a spiritual director. This way we can address those things where we have got stuck or have blind spots. To have someone to accompany us on this journey can help us learn and gain greater understanding. With the use of skilful questions and comments, they may also enable us to receive insight and revelation.

Renewing our minds is a continual process. It requires us to allow the Holy Spirit to shape our thinking in line with the mind of Christ.[8] I will be devoting a later chapter to re-wiring our thoughts to express the values of the kingdom. However, before I focus on this part of the call, there is something else that is required in the preparation. This is dealing with unfinished business.

These are the things that hang around that never really get transfigured by God's grace. They include disappointments that make our hearts sick[9], or the wounds that never quite get healed. Even when I think I am mending, it doesn't take much for the wound to break open again. Although these hurts are not physical, I wonder how much of my experience of migraine relate to this mind-body connection. Perhaps my emotional wounds need to be addressed before my body can fully heal. Bill Johnson writes:

'When our desires go unfulfilled, our bodies and spirits suffer together. One of the causes of sickness and disease is disappointment that is never dealt with redemptively. People go through a disappointing circumstance and never get before God to have Him heal the hurts they pour out from their soul. The physical body inevitably reflects what's going on.' [10]

This revelation makes me uncomfortable because I realise that I have been, and still am at times, a 'champion striver'. I look to improve myself through learning and effort, always seeking out others who I believe have greater knowledge or revelation than me. In some ways that is a humble position to take because I am always open to learning from others, but it can also be a way of procrastinating. We can play this game with God too. Instead of coming to Him directly, we go to others and ask help from them, believing that their hotline to God is better and more accurate than ours.

Many of us go *anywhere but God* at times. Prayer can become a last resort rather than a first response and we can seek insight from a host of others before Abba. I have profited from the accompaniment of a spiritual director and occasionally, a counsellor, but I also know that there are some things that I just have to lay at the foot of the cross myself. We all have defences that have been erected to protect us in some way. Part of the call to radical repentance involves us moving to a place, or perhaps it's more accurate to say - God *brings* us to that place, where we don't need these defences anymore. We give them to God and let Him do the healing work within us. It is a surrender; a recognition that I can't totally fix myself – and that is okay. It might even be the beginning of wisdom.

Settling myself down for some two-way journaling, I wrote to God about being my authentic self in my own shoes and letting go of all that was holding me back. I asked for His guidance, saying that I wanted to be healthy and free enough to be able to carry what He has for me and to be the new wineskin waiting for the new wine. I was prepared to be brave and face those wounds that never truly healed. I also had to accept the part I have played, often picking at the healing scabs and making them bleed again.

Out of the two-way process of writing to God and listening for His answers, I began to think about how we remember events. In situations of conflict, we tend to re-frame a memory to protect ourselves. This process then obscures our learning. It hampers our personal insight and compassion for the other because we have become inflexible in our defensive position. We see this when we remember things in a way that puts us in a good light and casts the blame elsewhere. We become stuck in our own analysis and then wonder why we can't let the conflict go without a demand for justification rising from within us: *'It isn't my fault', 'They are to blame', 'I am the victim here.'*

In some situations, this may be accurate. When a survivor speaks about abuse, it is a necessity to lay responsibility in the right place and to claim this truth. However, in most situations that provoke conflict, we discover more about ourselves and others when we are open to listening and learning and are committed to God's process within us.

After focusing on the power and presence of Jesus and asking Him to respond to the questions I posed, I got into the flow of writing. I didn't censor what I wrote or stop and start to assess it. I surrendered to the flow state within and wrote what came into my heart.[11]

'*CAN YOU FEEL THE BLOCKAGE, Mandy? The fact that you can is progress. It is revealed to you, but so is the remedy. Nothing can withstand My power – so it's time to release it to Me, holding nothing back. You cannot get the outcome you desire that you are completely understood, justified, and accepted by others. It is not possible while free will stands.*

This is the heart of the matter. You have been wanting something those who moved against you can't give - justification. Free will means you cannot control what they think of you. Putting the past to rest is only about you, not them. Let them think their own thoughts. Let them hold their own views - however unjust it may seem to you. Let them go.

You are still looking outside of yourself for validation. You are putting others' shoes on instead of wearing your own.

Repent of your control. Renounce your attempts to make you the hero and them the villain. This is not what freedom is about.

By all means - process your hurts, feel them, and then give them to Me. What you have been feeling is a whole load of pain with nowhere to put it. You must give others their freedom to choose and make sure your identity and self-esteem is separate from it. This is your work. You are not honouring them with the right to choose and this is what is keeping you bound. You want a simple truth that is jointly understood; clean, fair, and decisive. But only I have that vision. Only I see every mitigating circumstance and every character flaw, as well as strength. I do not give My children that vision because I call you to love, not to judge.

Love is when you step back allowing the other person to have the dignity of choosing their own viewpoint. You are respecting them as a human being and cutting yourself free from the consequences of those choices. This is the deathblow to co-dependency; this is the answer to unforgiveness.

I invite you to bring all your unfinished business to Me.

It is a lie that you, alone, can make everything okay and that thinking through things can 'solve' them. You may gain insights and revelation from doing that, and it's healthier to own your own feelings than to deny or repress them – but that is not the core problem. It will get you so far, learning to listen to yourself and validate your feelings, but in the end, it is giving respect to them to have the right to their own feelings that allows you to let go of control.

So, your healing is twofold. Giving up control over someone else's reactions, views, and story-telling details, and coming to Me for healing of your own pain.

This is about releasing, and not about picking it up again later. When you pick it up again you are saying that having your view is the 'correct' one and the most important thing in the process. You are giving your power to them and strengthening a connection that is already an unhealthy soul-tie.

Do not take the eye of approval and give it to someone else – that is idolatry. Keep it where it needs to be – with Me. It is Me who tells you who you truly are.

Being an ambassador is being consumed with the things of the kingdom. We are partners in this. Lean into your identity - who I say you are – every time you feel that twinge of wanting to control someone's behaviour or someone's concept of you.'

WHEN I READ THIS BACK, I was astounded. It felt like truth because it resonated within, but it was still uncomfortable. I saw how exhausted I had become doing it my way. I wanted to do the right thing and forgive but this Word shone a bright spotlight on what that really means; I wanted to control the narrative.

Showing respect and honour to the other human being meant allowing them to hold their views, even if I totally disagreed with them or felt the standpoint was untrue or morally questionable. Being free meant walking away without trying to change or manipulate them into agreeing with my version of events. It cut the cords that bound us together. I was no longer waiting for validation. I was taking back my power and putting on my own shoes.

As I engaged repeatedly with this Word, I began to feel hope rising within me. Without repeatedly exposing my vulnerable wounds or constantly picking at them - which is a sign of self-harm, they could get better. I could release both me and the other person from unforgiveness and it would bring freedom and healing to us both. I would then just have the scars to remind me.

Kris Vallotton, heard a prophetic word about God's treatment of scars on His children. In it, God says:

'I will not remove the scars from your life. Instead, I will rearrange them in such a way that they have the appearance of carving on a fine piece of crystal.' [12]

From another wing of the Church, Nadia Bolz-Weber writes about the importance of these scars. She says:

'Our pain and failure – the things we so often try to hide, the things that create shame, the things that scar – are what gives us texture. And without texture there is nothing for others to connect to.' [13]

On one hand speaking about this journey feels incredibly exposing. I am sharing the process in a way that makes me feel vulnerable. However, then I realise that having courage to share this story without heaping shame, guilt, or fear on my head, may be just the encouragement that someone else needs. It may inspire them to go on their own journey towards greater freedom.

We all have wounds and some of them are still unhealed. It is reassuring to know that these can become beautiful scars that show we are human and have survived. We have learned and grown and released, and in doing so we inhabit more freely the person we are called to be. Shawn Bolz sums it up:

'Regardless of our pasts, I think all of us end up coming to a place of needing to find more of our identity in Christ.' [14]

When we renounce the idolatry that puts something else in the way of where God should be and refocus on His eye of approval, we finally come home to who we are in Him. Then we discover, all over again, how good God is.

7

OFFENCE

e forgive, we mortify our resentment; a week later some chain of thought carries us back to the original offence and we discover the old resentment blazing away as if nothing had been done about it at all. We need to forgive our brother seventy times seven not only for 490 offences but for one offence.'

C. S. Lewis

'The kingdom comes when the finished work of Jesus is made visible, manifesting God's rule in our broken world.'

The Ambassador

I was in the refiner's fire. God was teaching me to

live from my authentic self and to bring to Him the unfinished business of my life. We had touched on the subject of forgiveness before but now God was bringing this to the forefront of our conversations. I had thought I could forgive by my own will power, but it turns out that I can't. Neither was I to control past narratives, ensuring they were always in my favour. It seems that only God gets to be judge in these circumstances, which is a shame, because I clearly thought I was good at it.

I discovered I could experience more freedom when I became more critically aware, and did things God's way, abdicating my role as judge and jury. Paradoxically, when I gave the other person the freedom to choose their own view of events, I found the same liberty myself. I was no longer tied to the person who wounded me. Forgiveness followed when the cord that bound me to my antagonist was cut and I could offer the situation, all my feelings, and the other person, to God.

This next chapter builds on the previous two. It focuses on learning how to avoid creating these situations in the first place. I had come to the conclusion that if I were serious about the challenge of fulfilling my role as an ambassador, then practising being *unoffended* was an important skill to learn.

I could see there were significant learning opportunities everywhere because the potential for being offended is all around us. Social media illustrates it perfectly. One only has to post or tweet an opinion to see others pile in to support or denigrate the viewpoint. Trolls post offensive responses. 'Twitter storms' rage. It all shows that offence is alive and well, provoking virtue signalling, polarising opinion, and fuelling heated online engagement. Social media platforms offer a popular arena where opinions are treated as facts, and where the whole world is invited to comment, usually in 280 characters or less. It is a showground for trading in offence.

Some people love it, seeing it as fun and provocative. They don't take it seriously. It offers the safety of distance, much like singing abuse at opposing fans in a football stadium. It's part of the atmosphere and the camaraderie with those on our team. It is because we are removed from it physically that we can be emboldened. If our opponent were right next to us, most of us would be unlikely to behave the same way. Social media provides both distance and potential anonymity, and this affects how we engage with others.

First, we need to be aware of what taking offence costs us. When we hold onto an offence, we filter everything through it.[1] It keeps us stuck, like a scratched vinyl record that plays the same section of music over and over again. It may consume us to the point that it's all we can think about and there's no relief when we repeat the story to whomever will listen, just a re-playing of the pain. It prevents us from experiencing the freedom that God wants to give us, because we are captive to our own inability to forgive. Over time it creates a parched wasteland within us. Heidi Baker writes:

'If you want to birth the miraculous, you cannot afford to waste time getting offended. Offense stops you carrying the promise to full term, and you really never know what God plans to do with a situation that offends you at first.' [2]

This tells us that God can work within us, redeeming the worst that humankind can do, but it comes back to us being partners with Him. In the Older Testament, Joseph the dreamer had a lot to be offended about. He was sold into slavery by his brothers, falsely accused of sexual assault by the wife of his boss, stripped of his authority and status in the household, thrown into prison and forgotten for two years, even by Pharaoh's cup bearer who he'd interpreted a dream for.[3] It would not be surprising if he had become bitter and twisted after all of that. However, God did a work of grace within Joseph because He needed to transform his character. Joseph's destiny was to carry the responsibility, wisdom, maturity, and insight to advise the most powerful ruler in the region, to save a whole nation from famine, and protect his birth family. This juvenile, self-absorbed, favourite son of Jacob would never have been able to do that, if he hadn't been through the refiner's fire. Joseph's two sons are named to bear witness to God's redemption in suffering. In the Genesis account, Joseph says he named his first son, Manasseh, *"it is because God has made me forget all my trouble and all my father's house-hold"* and, the second is named Ephraim, *"it is because God has made me fruitful in the land of my suffering."* [4] This is not about ignoring pain or pretending it doesn't hurt. It is about bringing it into the redemptive healing of the light of God, releasing it to Him and letting Him transform it for good. It makes the difference between becoming either a wounded healer or an unhealed wounder.

There are things that we should be offended at, like poverty, oppression, cruelty, and injustice. These things offend the heart of God because He is just. In the Bible, we have many examples showing how God is concerned with justice. He hears the voice of the oppressed and acts on it as He did when the Hebrews were slaves in Egypt[5]. He responds to the cries of Ishmael when he and his mother, Hagar, are driven out into the desert.[6] He also hears the blood cry out from the ground where Abel was murdered.[7] According to the Psalms, He is ready to intervene when He hears our distress[8] and we see this actualised perfectly in the ministry of Jesus.[9]

Alongside His desire for justice, God also shows mercy. He is a forgiving God, as He was when the Ninevites repented after receiving the grumpy, begrudging ministry of Jonah.[10] He may also still forgive when no repentance comes, such as when Jesus forgave His enemies on the cross.

'...*Father, forgive them, for they do not know what they are doing.*' [11]

This is always a surprising verse because, from the Biblical text, it looks as if every person who plotted against Jesus knew exactly what they were doing.[12] Despite Pilate's public hand washing, distancing himself from the event,[13] it was still the Roman system that put Jesus to death. Caesar was still the executioner and Pilate just acquiesced to Empire.

What those who condemned Jesus didn't know was they were putting the incarnate God on the cross. With that action, God the Son, demonstrated His solidarity with all suffering peoples. He embraced the pain so as to transform it, and broke the power of sin and death forever. As Nadia Bolz-Weber states:

'*God is always present in love and in suffering.*' [14]

This should be an encouragement when we are dealing with our wounds, even when we can't see or predict how it's going to work out. We can trust the redemptive power of God and know that He will find a way. He has done it already through the cross, but we have to see it applied to our timeline.

God's transforming work is depicted triumphantly in the Eastern Orthodox icon of *Anastasis*. Taking the inspiration from 1 Peter 4: 6, it shows the crucified Christ in Hades, standing on the broken gates of Hell. Satan is bound under His feet and all the keys of captivity are visible. With each hand, Jesus is pulling Adam and Eve out of their coffins into new life. They are a symbol of the redemption of all humanity. It is a graphic way of showing that, even in the quietness and desolation before Jesus visibly walks in the garden on the Sunday morning, God is breaking open the prisons where people have been held captive. It proclaims that suffering love is stronger than any other force in this world. It's a powerful icon of hope and resurrection signifying that the domination system's power is defeated by the higher way of love.

This can be seen through the Gospels and, most graphically, in Jesus' ministry of deliverance. The kingdom breaks in and displaces the inferior force of the domination system. Life evicts death, sickness is ousted by healing, forgiveness rubs out shame and guilt, and wholeness and salvation replace fragmentation and alienation. The kingdom comes when the finished work of Jesus is made visible, manifesting God's rule in our broken world. This may come through the miraculous, where things impossible are made possible, but it's also breaks through in the small moments of everyday life, through acts of kindness, gratitude, faith, and love.

While the works of evil originate from non-human-beings still have a choice in

how we respond to them. This is the necessary gift of
free will. However, if we are given the choice of what
position we take, how do we remain unoffended
when another has actively taken the side of evil?
There are clearly some situations that are not open
to debate. We may want to give others freedom to
have their choice, but some actions are indefensible
and some roads, once embarked on, are difficult to
turn back from. I am reminded of a line from Shakespeare's play, *Macbeth,* that illustrates how turning
back from a chosen path can be just as difficult, or
even more so, than continuing down it.

> *'I am in blood,*
> *Stepp'd in so far that, should I wade no more,*
> *Returning were as tedious as go o'er'* [15]

At times, nothing describes an action better than
the word 'evil'. It cannot be relativised. It is, what it
is, without mitigation. However, actions are different
from those who commit them. Jesus calls us to love
our enemies[16] but how do we recover the humanity
and divine image of that person when they are
colluding with the darkness and their actions are
unequivocally evil? Ephesians 6: 12 reminds us that:

> *'For our struggle is not against flesh and blood but*
> *against the rulers, against the authorities, against the*
> *powers of this dark world and against the spiritual forces*
> *of evil in the heavenly realms.'*

This is surely an encouragement to divide and
rule. We see the person as a child of God, made in

His image and with a God-given purpose available to them, but they, under the influence of malign forces, have chosen to go a different way. Choosing to see the good, original design in humanity[17] doesn't mean we are naïve about dangerous or damaging people, always believing the best when their behaviour indicates otherwise. We are called to be as shrewd as serpents, as well as innocent as doves.[18] We do not have to put ourselves in a position where we are abused again. Loving oneself is also about attending to our own boundaries and learning Godly wisdom.

Offence poisons everyone; the one who gives it and the one who takes it. When we hold offence in our hearts, we see ourselves as the victim and blame everyone who has hurt us. We justify our anger, bitterness, and resentment and all the other feelings that surface when we think about the offence.[19] Martyn Percy states:

'Anger can lead to bitterness which consumes and leads to narcissism.' [20]

This narcissism means we continually focus on ourselves, and we build walls around us for protection (which is different from maintaining healthy boundaries). We distrust the motives of others and major in self-preservation. John Bevere states that harbouring an offence keeps us from seeing our own character flaws because the blame is deferred to another. He writes:

'You never have to face your role, your immaturity, or your sin because you see only the faults of the offender.' [21]

Here is the comfort and relief in projecting everything onto the 'villain'. We retain our righteousness as we declare the other, the sinner. It is not surprising that Jesus told us to take the plank out of our eyes first, before we tried to address the speck in another's eye.[22] This image, according to Walter Wink, is the earliest known teaching of projection. The splinter in the other's eye is a chip off the same log that is in one's own eye. We see in the other what we could not see in ourselves. The log totally blinds us so we can see nothing objectively.[23]

Wink argues that it is our need for projection that makes it so difficult to love our enemies. By discharging our hatred on external targets, we can achieve a partial release from pent-up energy festering in the unconscious. The second reason he cites for this challenge, is perfectionism. This is one of the forms that narcissism takes. He writes:

'Perfectionism has a secret and unacknowledged need for enemies. Perfectionists are perfect only by comparison.' [24]

Despite the often translated 'be perfect, therefore, as your heavenly Father is perfect' of Matthew 5:48, there is no such word or even concept in Aramaic or Hebrew. The word is a Greek aesthetic term for a perfect geometric form or sculpture, not for moral perfection, which was considered beyond the grasp of human beings. [25]

The projection of all our unwanted *stuff* onto others gives the appearance that we are cleaner than we are. We are purer than *those people over there*, which must mean we are more worthy, and generally better than them. Although it's a nonsense, the insecurity driving these thoughts colours our communal church life and faith. Though we are explicitly warned off from judging and controlling, we do so anyway, consciously, and unconsciously.

Grappling with loving our enemies brings the question of offence and what to do with it into sharp focus. To combat our tendency to project, we must own those things within us which are uncomfort-able and unacceptable, dragging them into the light of God, to see and recognise them ourselves, and to offer them up to God. Walter Wink writes:

'if God is compassionate toward us, with all our unre-deemed evil, then God must treat our enemies the same way. As we begin to acknowledge our own inner shadow, we become more tolerant of the shadow in others. As we begin to love the enemy within, we develop the compas-sion we need to love the enemy without.' [26]

Nadia Bolz-Webber reminds us that the good news of the Gospel has to be good news for everyone otherwise it is just ideology,[27] and when we see Jesus crossing every cultural, political, social and religious boundary to draw people in, we see that demon-strated.

This reflection and my conversations with God, were helping me to look at how I could prevent a knee-jerk reaction into offence. In practical terms, I recognised there is value in purposefully slowing down my thinking in order to resist being offended. It is good to remind ourselves that the other person may not have meant to cause offence. They may have just been careless in their words or spoken from their own wounds and insecurities. These defensive strategies perform the function of protecting or bolstering the other person. They are not primarily about us. This revelation will help us not to take it personally, and may prevent an offence from taking hold. However, we still need to own our feelings, rather than deny them, and come to God for His healing and teaching.

When we are offended, we are given an insight into our own, and others,' vulnerabilities. With God's help, it is an opportunity to develop greater compassion and mercy, and to practise forgiveness. It is in our universal need for God that we realise that this is not a faith for the perfect, it is a faith for the forgiven.

8

BLESSING

'*B less more; blame less.*'

Marianne Williamson

'*...there is power in the spoken word when we are speaking what is in God's heart. It changes atmospheres and draws down from the heavenly dimension the reality of kingdom life.*'

The Ambassador

This period of reflection was tough. God had brought me to explore the emotional baggage I carried and to consider how I handled offence and forgiveness. This was the work of building and refining character and it wasn't very comfortable.

Although I longed to get on with the business of being an ambassador, I felt God was telling me there was one more major topic I needed to engage with in this part of the process. It was a positive and practical way of addressing the challenges outlined in the last three chapters and an important skill to have in an ambassador's repertoire. It was the subject of blessing.

Some years ago, I had the experience of finding a real enemy. A woman in the parish where I was the vicar *loathed* me. That may seem extreme, but sadly, it is true. It didn't matter what I did or didn't do, her attitude remained the same and it surfaced in behaviour I found challenging. She had been a long-standing resident in the parish and, because her vitriol wasn't aimed at everyone - just the vicar and a small handful of others, it was generally tolerated. She was seen as just one of those eccentric characters, common in small rural communities.

I didn't know what I had done to provoke such hatred and I found dealing with the situation painful. It did, however, teach me something about the practice of blessing our enemies. This is not me pretending to be super holy. The last thing I wanted to do was bless her, but I knew that I had to put some 'God space' between her and me.

It was clear from this woman's words and behaviour that she was determined to think badly of me and to interpret everything I said or did through that lens. She wouldn't recognise God's love reflected in my actions, however hard I tried to be His channel. Blessing her was not an attempt to manipulate her or bring her round to my way of thinking, because she had already made up her mind and I had to concede that I couldn't control how she perceived me.

Russ Parker, in his book, *Rediscovering the Ministry of Blessing,* argues that one of the benefits of blessing those who persecute us is that:

'...we may not be consumed by the scars of battle but transformed by the love of God that we share with them.'[1]

I found truth in this, because if I am blessing her, at least I'm not cursing her.

I could ask God to bring out His best in her, and for her. The pronouncement of God's heart for her was about reminding me that this woman was still a child of God, loved by God, and a fellow human-being. It was important to hold onto this because when we become locked into battle with those who oppose us, we find it energizing to de-humanise them and make them different from us. Then we can release our anger on them and feel justified in the counterattack. I didn't want to end up in this place, even if my 'injustice monitor' was sounding the alarm loudly and getting me ready to defend myself.

The second thing that the act of blessing did was help me gain some protection from the negativity that was coming my way. The Bible states that an undeserved curse doesn't come to rest[2], but it can still be a deeply unpleasant experience. If we get consumed by it, trying to argue against the mindset behind it, we give it energy. It feeds on our attention and it begins to colonise us. Like a cancer, it grows and metastasises, taking hold of our emotions and thought life when we shouldn't have given it house-room in the first place. Walter Wink writes:

'We become what we hate. The very act of hating something draws it to us. Since our hate is usually a direct response to an evil done to us, our hate almost invariable causes us to respond in the terms already laid down by the enemy. Unaware of what is happening, we turn into the very thing we oppose.' [3]

Part of us may want to get stuck into the fight with our enemies but it's not how we remain free. When we engage with the battle, it causes us to drift from our calling, it inflates our ego, and it polarises issues and people into camps. We lose part of our humanity where we no longer see the complexities of life, only the black and white of our own precon-ceived framework which, of course, we believe is always accurate. We are not able to learn from others, or to respond with wisdom, tact, skill, and nuance. Instead, we are likely to react automatically and with greater force than is necessary. This is because we often think that we must act strongly and fight fire with fire. We do not want to appear weak to our enemy. The problem is that returning fire only serves to embolden our opponent. They now have something concrete to fight against. This gives energy to the battle, as they define and strengthen themselves against us.

Pronouncing blessing is a way of circumventing this cycle of retaliation and violence. It gives us freedom to act so that we do not become like those who oppose us. Blessing takes the heat out of the battle, leaving no opponent to fight. The aggressor is left standing alone, with pride and courage slowly deflating, or anger burning itself out. I have found that staying in a place of blessing, rather than coun- terattacking from anger, has the advantage of making the other person appear vindictive or foolish if they continue - at least in the court of public opin- ion. It is a long game, but it's worth playing it, if it means we evade the bitterness that follows these kinds of protracted conflicts.

The Apostle Paul writes to the Roman Christians telling them not to be overcome by evil but to over- come evil with good.[4] He quotes from the book of Proverbs saying:

'If your enemy is hungry, feed him; if he is thirsty, give him something to drink. In doing this, you will heap burning coals on his head.' [5]

This is not to be interpreted as an act of revenge causing scalds and burns. Quite the opposite. When curses are met with blessing, it may lead our enemies to burn with shame at their original behaviour. Kindness therefore can have the effect of leading someone to repentance, and ashes on the forehead are often an image of that.

Another helpful strategy in these circumstances is to make sure we can see the bigger picture. Having an enemy in our sights narrows our field of vision. We are so locked into the conflict that it distorts what we see and hear, and if we brood on it, it becomes magnified in every part of our life.

This reminded me of what I had learned about chronic pain in my previous book, *The Beach*. The more I had focused on my pain, the more attention and energy I gave to it, and the more severe my headaches became. When I was able to relax, to tell myself that I was okay, I was safe and there was no danger, the better able I was to let go of the tension in my body and the fear in my mind. Consequently, I found that the pain in my head reduced too.

Making sure that we do things in our life other than dwell on an uncomfortable situation gives us some form of relief from its intensity. Putting the current battle within the framework of our wider faith is helpful too. I've always found it good to remind myself of Mother Teresa's prayer, *The Final Analysis*. It doesn't hide from the realities of our disappointments and struggles but puts them into a framework that helps us to remember what our main priority is.

*'People are often unreasonable, irrational, and
self-centred.
Forgive them anyway.
If you are kind, people may accuse you of selfish,
ulterior motives.
Be kind anyway.
If you are successful, you will win some unfaithful
friends and some genuine enemies.
Succeed anyway.
If you are honest and sincere people may deceive
you.
Be honest and sincere anyway.
What you spend years creating, others could destroy
overnight.
Create anyway.
If you find serenity and happiness, some may be
jealous.
Be happy anyway.
The good you do today, will often be forgotten.
Do good anyway.
Give the best you have, and it will never be enough.
Give your best anyway.
In the final analysis, it is between you and God.
It was never between you and them anyway.'* [6]

Pronouncing blessing helps us to stay connected
to God and not just in the challenging times when
people oppose us. I discovered more about the
ministry of blessing when a group of us from my
home parish went to the retreat centre in West

Wales, called Ffald-y-Brenin. We had read the book
The Grace Outpouring by Roy Godwin, who at the
time was running the centre with his wife, Daphne.
Roy wrote about the extraordinary effect that
blessing had on the community there, and the visitors who came, including those who weren't sure
that God even existed. Story after story testified to
the way that God just broke in with His sovereign
power. All Roy and Daphne usually did was make
the visitors a cup of tea, talk about the centre, show
them around, bless them, and leave them in the
small chapel for a little while. It wasn't a flashy
conference centre endorsed by famous names with
big international ministries. There was no heavy
sell, or long worship service. This was just God
meeting people again and again in power in this
little rural outpost on a windy, Welsh hillside.

   One of the distinctions Godwin makes is that
blessing isn't about intercession. They didn't pray for
God to bless; they were *speaking out* blessings in the
name of Jesus. There is no expectation on the person
receiving blessing to believe in God or wait for God
to do something. Roy Godwin writes:

   *'Blessing someone is simple and easy. The Holy Spirit
comes because when you bless you are reflecting something that the Father is doing and speaking words that
the Father desires to be said.'* [7]

   When God instructed Moses to explain to Aaron
how the priests were to act, pronouncing blessing

over the people was part of it, along with intercession.[8] It is about exercising faith and pronouncing
what aligns with God's heart. We are coming into
agreement with the blessing and speaking it out
boldly, and we know that when we speak God's
words, they do not return to Him empty but accomplish what they were meant to.[9] It means that there
is power in the spoken word when we are speaking
what is in God's heart. It changes atmospheres and
draws down from the heavenly dimension the reality
of kingdom life. Roy and Daphne Godwin discovered the reality of this at Ffald-y-Brenin. Roy writes:

*'Somehow we release something here on earth when
we're acting in unison with the cry of heaven. The
kingdom is released when there's an agreement between
heaven and earth. His will can be done on earth, just as it
is in heaven.'* [10]

When we visited Ffald-y-Brenin in 2017 we were
surprised to see how remote it was. It was small and
didn't have a lot of resources. The book shop area
was tiny, and the chapel was also a fraction of the
size of our home church. Despite all of this, we could
tell it was a special place; a *thin* place where one can
feel heaven touching earth more tangibly. The
welcome and the food were fabulous and the
blessing on arrival set the course for the next couple
of days. Sadly, we couldn't stay long, and the weather
was challenging. Yet even in this couple of days
break, God seemed to be ahead of us. We prayed for

one of our group, who had suffered an injury from a skiing accident. When she returned and went to see her consultant, it was found that her leg had healed, and the consultant said that he'd never known one of those types of injuries to be healed without surgery.

On our return, we were keen to start the practice of blessing as part of our Morning and Evening Prayer. Each day we now speak out blessings on the community, the church, on individuals, on the world, or more generally, for spiritual growth. It also has become part of our prayer ministry with those in need. Pronouncing blessing illustrates the generosity of God for all His creation and His desire to show mercy on us, through healing, forgiveness, and restoration.

We pronounce blessings on people, but also on the land. This pattern was established in Ffald-y-Brenin, when the team were called to pray in the name of Jesus and press His blood into the land, so it covered every curse, every sin, and every other form of bloodshed that had happened in the past.[11] Russ Parker, in his book, *Healing Wounded History – reconciling peoples and healing places* also writes about its benefits on the physical environment. He writes:

'Throughout scripture we are taught that there is a direct connection between human story and the land or ground on which this story occurs...One of the recurring

threads ...is the connection between forgiveness of the sins of the nation and a restored connection with the land.' [12]

Parker argues that the land itself has the capacity to hold, reflect and repeat the unhealed stories between people as if they were sown into the soil. The importance and power of memories has a shaping influence over communities in their identity and group story. God, therefore, calls us into a place to be part of the ministry of reconciliation through confession and repentance, to bring deliverance to that which is stuck in a repeated pattern. Even though the bloodshed, division or betrayal may have happened many centuries before, we can still bring change through representational confession.

The concept of representational confession is controversial. Opponents question whether we can genuinely represent others in such a confession when we are removed in time and space from them and therefore are not speaking directly for them. However, there may be some benefits in pursuing this course. We may accept some form of corporate responsibility for past events, and express solidarity with those who have suffered. It is a sign of sorrow and lament and that, in itself, may be enough to move the process of reconciliation on within hurting communities. God will bless our efforts because reconciliation matters to Him. It is on His heart for people to be reconciled to one another[13] just as Jesus is the reconciler between us and God. This is central to our understanding of being Christ's ambassadors.

'...All this is from God, who reconciled us to himself through Christ and gave us the ministry of reconciliation: that God was reconciling the world to himself in Christ, not counting people's sins against them. And he was committed to us the message of reconciliation. We are therefore Christ's ambassadors, as though God were making his appeal through us.' [14]

This reconciliation with God impacts the personal, social, political, and cosmological aspects of life. God has brought this about, not through the law, but by Jesus Christ. The task of the church is to be the instrument of reconciliation in the world.[15] What Paul teaches is, that whatever frailty we have in our human nature or whatever inner turmoil we experience, nothing can thwart us from receiving the love God offers in Jesus Christ.[16] The Ministry of Blessing is one way we can demonstrate this.

9

COURSE CORRECTION

'No one longs for what he or she already has, and yet the accumulated insight of those wise about the spiritual life suggests that the reason so many of us cannot see the red X that marks the spot is because we are standing on it.'

Barbara Brown Taylor

'Others will make their own decisions about our king according to how we represent Him. This brings an immediacy to the topic. What we believe and transmit to the world is expressed via our words and behaviour. Whether we mean to or not, we leak our faith. This is not the signal to try harder, but to lean into grace.'

The Ambassador

When I wrote *The Beach* the chapters often followed a dream that I had, but this book has been different. What I have written here is not a dream, but still a response to a 'God incident'. It has been something I have sensed from the Holy Spirit or read. It still feels that I am building the bridge as I walk across it, responding immediately to the twists and turns of direction. I asked my spiritual director to read over what I had written and give me feedback so we could have a conversation about what I was learning.

One of the points he raised is about my *becoming* an ambassador. This is not what the text says. What I have written about in the previous chapters *is* a formation, but it's not specifically about becoming an ambassador. It's about maturing in my faith so that I can let go of what has weighed me down and run the race better.[1] What Paul writes in his second letter to the Corinthians is

'We **are** therefore Christ's ambassadors, as though God were making his appeal through us. We implore you on Christ's behalf: be reconciled to God.'[2]

There is no *becoming*. We *are* ambassadors already. Others will make their own decisions about our king according to how we represent Him. This brings an immediacy to the topic. What we believe and transmit to the world is expressed via our words and behaviour. Whether we mean to or not, we leak our faith. This is not the signal to try harder, but to lean into grace.

My director observed that my writing expressed many conditional statements. IF I did 'X', THEN God would do 'Y'. He challenged me about where the grace of God came into the equation. This is a fair point.

There are verses in the Bible that speak of God's actions in conditional terms.[3] The one that often comes to mind is from 2 Chronicles 7: 14. In it we read:

'IF my people, who are called by my name, will humble themselves and pray and seek my face and turn from their wicked ways, THEN I will hear from heaven, and I will forgive their sin and will heal their land.'

These 'if – then' promises put responsibility on us to fulfil conditions before the promised blessings come. This contractual way of thinking is part of our lives. When faced with choices, we often think about the question 'what's in it for me?' We might wrap it up in less egocentric terminology, but it amounts to the same thing. Rewards and sanctions motivate us. This is because so much of our normal life is regulated by 'if-then' thinking. *'If I want to pass my exams then I should waste less time and study more'; 'if I want to lose weight then I should take more exercise or eat less'; 'if I want to learn to play the piano well then I should practise more.'* All of these are true. These are choices and each has a consequence. What we choose will usually determine the result. Most of us are brought up with this kind of thinking and we bring our own children up to think this way too.

This reminds me of a token system that Patrick, my husband, and I instigated to manage the behaviour of our two sons when they were very young. Each child could earn 'glass nuggets' for clearly defined, positive, behaviour. It also followed that tokens could be lost by the choices that they made. This reward/sanction system was intended to make life manageable and teach two lively pre-school boys about sowing and reaping. This was essential at a time when their cognitive development meant that they didn't always recognise the dangers of their actions. They may have wanted to run to the playground, but they needed to wait for supervision to cross the road first. It also gave the opportunity to learn about behaving in social situations or to observe bedtime, both of which were more to do with their parents' mental wellbeing than the boys' safety. When a specified number of tokens were earned in the week, they could have a lucky dip in a bag of little toys. Behaviour-management techniques may look like bribery, but it worked in making them more biddable, and compliance is a highly rated quality when managing home, work, and two young children. I remember the day when one of our sons lost all the glass nuggets he had accumulated that week. He wailed in protest, but it taught the lesson he needed to learn. Behaviour has consequences. You reap what you sow.

This law of sowing and reaping is expressed in scripture[4] but there are universal promises too which are not connected to a condition. One of these is when Jesus says He will never leave or forsake us. The problem with focusing on the 'if – then' promises, is that we dilute grace, the unconditional, unmerited love of God. Grace is a gift that costs everything for the giver and nothing for the recipient[5] and that is at the heart of the Gospel. It works against conditionality because it means that we don't receive what we deserve. This is illustrated in the parable of the prodigal son.[6] I wrote about this parable in *The Beach* in reference to our sense of identity, but it's worth returning to this story in more detail to illustrate, not only the depth of God's grace, but the relationship between the undeserved love of God and the law of sowing and reaping.

This is such a familiar story to many that it's easy to miss the cultural significance of what is going on. First, the son who wants his inheritance is not just a young man desiring to get out into the world and spread his wings. This is a story of offence and shame. Within traditional cultures of the Middle East, a son coming to his father, demanding his inheritance, would be unthinkable. It would be an

outrage and an insult to the father and family.[7]
Henri Nouwen states: -

*'It is a heartless rejection of the home in which the
son was born and nurtured and a break with the most
precious tradition carefully upheld by the larger community of which he was a part. When Luke writes, "and left
for a distant country,"...[this is] about a drastic cutting
loose from the way of living, thinking, and acting that
has been handed down to him from generation to generation as a sacred legacy. More than disrespect, it is a
betrayal of the treasured values of family and community. The "distant country" is the world in which everything considered holy at home is disregarded.'* [8]

The son's actions are a rejection of his family. It
could force them to liquidate their estate early, but
the son doesn't care if his father dies, or his family
loses their farm. He just wants to enjoy life on his
terms.[9] According to the biblical scholar, Kenneth
Bailey, the cultural mores would expect that any
father faced with this demand would respond forcefully. He is supposed to take his left hand, (which is
symbolically worse than his right) and the back of
his hand, (worse than the front) and strike his son
across the face and drive him out of the house.[10]
However, this is not what the father does in the story.
Instead, he divides the property as requested. The
young man needs cash to go on his travels and so he
must sell the property to get it. Many in his community wouldn't want to buy it because of the shame

attached to it. The breakdown of the relationship is now public. It is likely that only someone on the fringe of the community would be willing to buy from the son in these circumstances.

Bailey states that a better translation of the Greek is that the son wastes his money in 'expensive,' rather than 'wild', living. The accusation of spending it on prostitutes comes from the elder brother later in the story, not in the initial text itself. The young man's situation becomes so wretched that he ends up feeding pigs in a distant country. Jews would not have farmed animals that are considered culturally 'unclean', so it's clear that he is in a Gentile, or non-Jewish, land. This is significant for two reasons. First, it shows how desperate he has become, and secondly, the specifics of his situation further cut him off from his home community,

Any young man who marries an immoral woman, or who loses the family inheritance among the Gentiles (as the younger son has), will face the *Kezazah* ceremony if he returns to his village. This is a 'cutting off' rite, which involves the villagers taking a large earthenware pot, filling it full of burned nuts and charred corn, and breaking it in front of the person. They call out his name and declare that he is cut off from his people. After which, no one will have anything to do with him.[11] The younger son would have known that this ceremony was threatening and so this reduces his options.

Much has been made of the younger son's repentance, but Bailey challenges this assumption. The young man does not say *'I have broken my father's heart'* or *'I'm sorry I've lost the money and brought shame on my family.'* He says the equivalent of *'I want to eat.'* [12] He also doesn't consider going back to be a slave in the household; instead, he plans to become a 'hired servant'[13] He wants some job training from his father and, even if he can't stay in the village due to the kezazah ceremony, he will be able to go elsewhere to be hired out and earn money to pay back the inheritance. Jesus tells the crowd what the young man was planning to say when he went home. He had prepared and practised the phrase *"Father I have sinned against heaven and against you."* For the Scribes who knew their scripture and were listening to the story, this would have echoes of Pharaoh's words to Moses in Exodus 10: 16. Here Pharaoh is trying to manipulate Moses to get him to call off the latest plague, but with no intention of letting the Israelites go. This echo is not accidental. It reveals the young man's thinking has nothing to do with repentance. This 'coming to his senses' in verse seventeen isn't the conviction of sin with the desire to make amends; it's about waking up to his situation and figuring out what card to play that gives him the best options.[14]

He knows that he is likely to get a brutal reception and he is planning to pay back the value of the inheritance, but that reveals how lost he is. He thinks the issue is about the money. He doesn't realise that this is about the family, the father's broken heart and the rejection of his love. Bailey states:

'the agony of rejected love is the deepest pain known to the human spirit.' [15]

The young man is only thinking in terms of seeing himself as a servant before a master, who has broken a law. He doesn't understand that he is a son before a compassionate father. The father, on the other hand, knows that when the young man fails and comes back that he will face eviction from the community. He goes against the cultural expectations of the head of a family and hoists up his robes to run down the road to embrace and kiss his son. It is a *'costly demonstration of unexpected love.'* [16]

Bailey states that this is where the young man must decide whether he is *found* or not.

The lost sheep being found and carried on the shoulders of the shepherd[17] was a symbol of repentance in the Early Church. If the young man agrees to *being found*, he must surrender his own ideas about how he is going to solve the problem.[18] He has to let the father do it for him, and we see that the father welcomes him with a party and reinstates his identity and authority as a son.[19] This is grace at work. The father bears the cost of the son's behaviour and the shame and damage to the family's reputation, and freely, without condition, gives back to him all that has been lost.

His other son is holding fast onto the law of sowing and reaping, believing that this wayward layabout deserves to be thrown out after the shame he's brought on the family name. He hears that there is a celebration of *shalom*. This is more than a party; this is a reconciliation. The older brother is furious with his father for showing such leniency and forgiveness. He refuses to join the party, and this rejection is a deep insult to his father. Bailey writes:

'The older son's response is crucially significant. He refused to enter the banquet hall where the guests have already arrived. In any social situation, banquet or no banquet, the male members of the family must come and shake hands with the guests even if they don't stay and visit. They cannot stay aloof if they are anywhere in the vicinity of the house. Failure to fulfil this courtesy is a personal insult to the guests and to the father, as host. The older son knows this and thereby his action is an intentional public insult to his father.' [20]

It's interesting that while the older brother is declaring that actions must have consequences, he is unable to see how his behaviour is as offensive as his brother's, as he snubs his father in public in front of all the community. It illustrates that we may be quick to uphold the law of sowing and reaping when it relates to others, but we often have blind spots when it comes to our own behaviour.

The father once again acts with grace. Instead of ignoring the older brother and dealing harshly with him later, as his culture expected, he humiliates himself by going out to his elder son to plead with him to join the reconciliation. This son is lost too, but he is refusing to be found. He calls the new arrival, 'this son of yours'[21] because he cannot bear to claim him as his brother. He is trapped in a jealous, judgmental, and self-righteous mindset. He begrudges his father's generosity and hates his brother. The father, however, shows the same forgiveness and love for him as his younger son, reminding him *you are with me always and everything I have is yours.*'[22] This is a call to remember that he can enjoy the powers and privileges of being a son any time. He can share and receive from the open hand and heart of his father whenever he wants to, but the elder son doesn't see it. His jealousy, resentment, and anger blind him to his father's goodness.

The elder son is acting like an orphan without identity and authority. He can only see resources as something that are competed for. When he hears that the fatted calf has been slaughtered to provide a lavish feast for his brother, he burns with the injustice of it. To his mind, this 'waster' has forfeited the right to such a party, and in comparison, he resents the meagre goat meal that he never had with his friends. Even though he stayed with the father, the elder son is a prodigal too, but in his heart.

It is perhaps telling that we never learn what the elder brother's response is in the story. It is left as a question and a challenge to the crowd. Telling this parable would have sparked discussion about what happened next. Does the older brother continue to smoulder with resentment? Or does he discover the grace that the father offers both sons? Would there have been a reconciliation between the brothers? There would have also been plenty of conversation about the role of the father. He had acted in a way that went against cultural expectations. Why did he do this? Was this a sign of weakness or unconditional love? As in most stories Jesus told, it would have left the crowd perplexed, wondering, arguing, exploring, and occasionally discovering, something new about the truth of God and His kingdom.

We know this as *The Parable of the Prodigal Son*, but it should be renamed *The Parable of the Two Lost Sons and the Compassionate Father* due to the story's focus. Although both sons are lost in their own ways, it is the character of the father that is the constant. Jesus tells this story to show us what Abba is really like. We need to be reminded of this because we have the propensity to project onto God our own desires and cultural characteristics. We make God in our own image, so He can approve of our choices and prejudices. This is a parable that cuts across all cultural expectations to show the unconditional love at the heart of God. Henri Nouwen writes:

'*The parable of the prodigal son is a story that speaks about a love that existed before any rejection was possible and that will still be there after all rejections have taken place. It is the first and everlasting love of a God who is Father as well as Mother. It is the fountain of all true human love, even the most limited. Jesus' whole life and preaching had only one aim: to reveal this inexhaustible, unlimited motherly and fatherly love of his God and to show the way to let that love guide every part of our daily lives...It is the love that always welcomes home and always wants to celebrate.*' [23]

Reflecting on this story, we can see a bigger truth emerging. The younger son wasn't as repentant as we are often taught, and the elder son was as disrespectful to his father in the end as his brother was. Both rejected their father's love and behaved in an offensive manner to him. Within the culture, the sons would expect a punitive reaction from the head of the family, but the father did the opposite. He moved through the pain of rejection into the forgiving grace where he was prepared to humiliate himself openly in public to reach out to them. He went out to seek the lost so they could be found and come back into the place of love, honour, and authority. We cannot read this parable without remembering the story of salvation and why the Gospel is good news.

Jesus tells it this way to show us that this is what God the Son does for us too. He leaves his home and His status and power and humbles Himself by becoming human.[24] He lives the life of love and service with us[25] and becomes obedient even to death on a cross. He scorns its shame[26] because even in our unrepentant state, He thinks that we are worth dying for.[27] He longs to find us and bring us home. This is why it's good to be reminded of how amazing grace is because the memories we have of reaping what we sow, and the demands of religion erode it. Even when we start with grace, salvation by works often creeps in. Before long there are hoops to go through, hurdles to jump over, and obstacles to navigate around on our way back home.

The problem is that grace feels alien to us because there is something counter-intuitive about it. We haven't earned it (so it's at odds with a meritocracy) and neither do we deserve it (as if it were an entitlement.) We are given it as a gift of love with no strings attached and we can't deal with that. We may become suspicious, wondering what the catch is. Or perhaps we become fearful, anxious that it will be withdrawn due to something we have done, just like our son discovered when he lost all the glass nuggets. The truth, however, is that there is nothing that we can do to make God love us more, or to make God love us less. It is there as a constant in our lives, but also a challenge to know what that means and how we live it out.

David Seamands knows all about this. Reflecting on his career as a counsellor, he saw some repeated themes in his work with Christians. He noted that the two major causes of most emotional problems were the failure to understand, receive, and live out God's unconditional grace and forgiveness; and the failure to give out that unconditional love, forgiveness, and grace to other people. He states:

'We read, we hear, we believe a good theology of grace. But that's not the way we live. The good news of the Gospel of grace has not penetrated the level of our emotions.' [28]

Even in the New Testament we see the slide away from grace. The Apostle Paul argues with the disciples in Galatia because having started with freedom, they began to slide backwards into the rules and regulations of the Law. He says:

'You were running a good race. Who cut in on you to keep you from obeying the truth?' [29]

He calls them to see they are not operating in the freedom Christ has for them.

I wonder whether part of this backsliding is because we are frightened of freedom, whereas rules and regulations at least give us structure. The decisions we make may provoke critical reactions in others, because there are always those who are threatened by our freedom and who wish to exert control over us, telling us we're wrong, bad, or mad. Paul pushes back in strong terms against this kind of criticism. He writes in Galatians:

'It is for freedom that Christ has set us free. Stand firm, then, and do not let yourselves be burdened again by a yoke of slavery.' [30]

Sadly, religion has been in the forefront of what Philip Yancey calls *ungrace*. Despite good intentions, control has often eclipsed freedom and grace has receded, while the law of sowing and reaping gains prominence. Behavioural management systems are created, where we earn the equivalent of glass nuggets for being good or lose them for falling short. It inevitably creates a tier system of righteousness and practising our faith becomes about us, and what we do, not God, and what He has already done, in Jesus. Nadia Bolz-Weber, writing about sexual ethics, writes:

'purity is easier to regulate than holiness. Our purity systems, even those established with the best of intentions, do not make us holy. They only create insiders and outsiders...Purity most often leads to pride or to despair, not to holiness. Because holiness is about union with, and purity is about separation from.' [31]

The law of sowing and reaping still has relevance because our actions have consequences, but what this course correction was showing me is that grace must always come first. It must be the central focus of who we are as people, not for anything we have done, but because of who God is and what He has done for us. We don't take grace and cheapen it, by seeing it as license to do whatever we want, because we know God loves us and will forgive us. The Apostle Paul slams that idea.[32] Instead, we are to mature in our faith, bear with one another in our disagreements and not let the expression of our freedom become a stumbling block to our neighbour.[33] Paul's summary principle is to seek what helps and builds up and promote the advantage of the Other. Kenneth Bailey puts it like this:

'freedom must be marinated with love' [34]

So where does this leave us? Having started at the beginning of this chapter with the truth that we *are* God's ambassadors rather than we *will be* at some future point, how has the journey down the rabbit hole of grace made a difference to our thinking? It reminds us that our starting point is always the unconditional love of God, not our own striving. We don't have to work hard to represent our king; the inherent goodness and holiness of all He has made is already a given. We are just drawing attention to it. We are recognising that God has already reconciled the world to Himself, through Jesus. He has done all the work and we, as His children, live in the good of it. This is the point of grace: it cost Him everything and us nothing, so that we could be set free. That's how good and loving our God is. Living with that freedom is something we must work out in each case, but when we marinate it with love, as Bailey puts it, we best represent our king.

Barbara Brown Taylor writes:

'Whoever you are, you are human. Wherever you are, you live in the world, which is just waiting for you to notice the holiness in it. So welcome to your own priesthood, practiced at the altar of your own life. The good news is that you have everything you need to begin.' [35]

10

GORDIAN KNOTS

'*The greatest need of our time is to clean out the enormous mass of mental and emotional rubbish that clutters our minds*'

Thomas Merton

'*The unmerited, unconditional love of God is the starting point in our faith. Jesus as the embodiment of this is the foundation on which everything else is built.*'

The Ambassador

The term 'Gordian knot' comes from a legend about Alexander the Great. The story goes that in 333 B.C. Alexander marched his army into the Phrygian capital of Gordium. There he came across a wagon tied with a knot so tightly entangled that it was difficult to see how the ropes might be separated. Local tradition said that the wagon once belonged to Gordius, the father of King Midas. An oracle declared that anyone who could unravel the knot was destined to become ruler of all Asia. According to the story, Alexander attempted to untie the knot by hand but was not successful. He then declared that it made no difference how the ropes were untied, so he drew his sword and sliced the knot in half. [1] The legend therefore lends the phrase 'Gordian knot' to denote a complex problem that is solved by a bold, simple solution.

I was thinking about Gordian knots because of the way I had become tangled up in the law of sowing and reaping at the expense of the superiority of grace. After studying the story we know as the Parable of the Prodigal Son, I felt I wanted to dig even deeper into the subject of grace and reflect on its implications. The unmerited, unconditional love of God is the starting point in our faith. Jesus as the embodiment of this is the foundation on which everything else is built. Because we live with so many conditional messages, this shift requires new thinking. We cannot earn grace or deserve it. We cannot work towards it, as if we could make it ours by a process of gradual possession. Instead, it is a gift that is given to us. But gifts, by definition, only come into being when they are accepted. An unwanted or unclaimed gift belongs to no one. This underlines the fact that to operate under grace, we must receive and accept it, allowing ourselves to be found by God. There is no pleading, bargaining or persuasion required. It is a profound offering of love from Abba, through the person of Jesus, in the power of the Holy Spirit. This is not the untangling of the strands; this is the sword slicing through the knot. This is what the parable of the two lost sons and the compassionate father is all about.

What this starting point requires is our dependence on God and what He offers us. We are emptied of our self-sufficiency and our need to control through our own efforts. In the story Jesus tells, the father, representing God, does not wait for the prodigal to come to him but rather at great cost goes out to find and resurrect the one who is lost and dead. Kenneth Bailey writes that these actions, seen in a Middle Eastern context, clearly affirm one of the deepest levels of the meaning of both the incarnation and the atonement.[2] God, the Holy Trinity, does the work; we get the benefit. God reconciles the world to Himself, and we become ambassadors of that message of reconciliation. What an honour and a privilege it is to proclaim the saving action of God. What a relief it is to declare that there are no winners or losers among us, only those who have claimed the gift, and those who have yet to do so. How humbling it is to know that this cost God everything, but He did so because He thinks we are worth it. We don't arrive at these conclusions through a process of deliberation or weighing up the arguments. The sword of truth slices through the knot and there is a jolt as the pressure of earning our way before God is released and we discover freedom.

I have written earlier in this book about our misplaced identity where I used the metaphor of wearing borrowed shoes. Now, after reflecting further on grace and the law of sowing and reaping, I want to revisit the subject of how we live from our God-given identity and let go of false images. It is not enough to say living authentically is a challenge; we want to consider how it may be achieved and how it relates to the story of the Gordian knot.

In this chapter, I'm going to use a different metaphor; one of looking at our reflection in a mirror. Despite knowing that we are God's children, we easily drift back to believe that who we are is defined by what the world has told us. Like the law of sowing and reaping, we have been taught about ourselves through our own socialisation. Our value has been defined through our cultural privileges and prejudices, and by our family beliefs and systems. When we are children, our family and community hold up a mirror through which we see ourselves. Although this is regarded as a true reflection of us, there is plenty of scope for distortion and lies. The presence of such misleading impressions make the reflection's accuracy questionable, and yet most of us believe that what we see in their mirror must depict a correct likeness of who we are. To challenge the image represented by our family or community triggers disapproval. What the system cannot control or accept, it will reject and eject[3] and being at the end of that is a painful place to be.

Therapy can help us find our authentic selves. It can give a respite from the enduring message that we are who our family or community say we are. One therapist, Rebecca Mandeville, treats clients who have taken on false identities due to abuse within families. Using the analogy of the Gordian knot, she advocates a robust approach to the distortions that have affected her clients' sense of self. She states:

'I encourage clients to consider the possibility that they can dis-identify from the 'shaming and blaming' stories directed at them via 'slicing through' to the truth of who they actually are.' [4]

Critics may argue that it is arrogant or delusional to completely reject the image that we see of ourselves in the world's mirror. They propose that there may be some reflections from others that are important for us to hold onto, especially those less than flattering ones that we'd rather not see. It gives us an appreciation of our full humanity; our shadow side and weaknesses, as well as our strengths. This may be true but it's my experience that a functioning relationship with the Holy Spirit can fulfil this role, and convict us of sin when necessary. Through the

work of the Spirit, we aren't battered with accusa-
tions (that's not from God) or made to feel ashamed
(that's not God either.) We are, however, drawn into a
place where we can see that we have missed the
mark and it's time to make amends. Too often we
confuse this gentle conviction or the check in our
Spirit, with the beating up that comes from other
sources that don't originate with God. Blake Healy
explains that there are lies that are total fabrications
and there are others that have a grain of truth in
them. We can often think that we must take on
everything that may have a grain of truth in it to be
open to growth and development, but that's not
usually helpful. He writes:

*'Looking for truth in the enemy's lies is like trying to
find a penny at the bottom of a barrel of broken glass:
painful and not worth the reward. It does not matter if a
lie is rooted in truth, has a grain of truth, or is 99 percent
true; if the enemy said it, then it will not be helpful to
you.'* [5]

Instead, we rely on the God who knows our
hearts and any offensive way in us and can lead us
onto the right path.[6] God's correction does not bring
condemnation but the opportunity to learn and
grow. He is the one who can provide the truth and
the power to be transformed. This is why, when it
comes to reflections, the most reliable image of
ourselves is the one we see mirrored in Abba's eyes.
It is our God-given identity, not one that has been

distorted through the painful experiences of our lives. To gain a sense of our true self requires us to come into a place of intimacy with God. Richard Rohr writes about the centrality of mirroring and reflecting, stating:

'The all-important thing is that you find the right mirror that mirrors you honestly and at depth. All personhood is created in this process and our job is always to stay inside this mirroring...our task is to trustfully receive and then reflect back the inner image transmitted to us until, as the apostle Paul expressed "we are gradually turned into the image that we reflect."...This is the whole spiritual journey in one sentence! All love, goodness and holiness is a reflected gift.' [7]

Rohr states that all authentic knowledge of God is participatory knowledge.[8] It is not logical knowledge. Therefore, if we are to cut through the Gordian knot of all that we have been told about ourselves and receive the identity of who God says we are, we do so by getting into the receiving line of God's love. This is not about ritual; this is about intimacy.

To foster the awareness and closeness of God, Rohr advocates the practice of contemplation. He describes this as learning how to abide in, and with, the Holy Spirit.[9] The Apostle Paul reminds the church in Corinth that our bodies are the Temple of the Holy Spirit,[10] and Rohr also draws a comparison to us being like the Ark of the Covenant in the Older Testament, the container of the sacred tablets of the

Ten Commandments.[11] Both images remind us that we already have within us the sacred Presence and we are changed by allowing and appreciating that felt experience to take hold.

Jesus encourages us to contemplate in His teaching about keeping worry at bay. He instructs us to look at the birds of the air and to consider the flowers growing in the field.[12] This contemplation leads us to remember God's provision and care for all His Creation and this calms the anxiety within. We have another example of this in Luke's gospel when we read that Mary treasured in her heart all the events and circumstances of Jesus' early life, making powerful memories to remind her of the significance of all that she'd experienced.[13]

Being present in the moment helps us to stay grounded. It enables us to cherish each moment and release anxious thoughts about the past and the future, freeing up the mental space we clutter up with our over-thinking. It is this mindfulness that brings relief and creates a stillness within that helps us more easily to connect with God's presence. This is a discipline that doesn't rely on everything else in our life being calm and tranquil. When the Psalmist exhorts us to *Be Still and Know that I AM God*' [14] it is when the earth gives way, the mountains fall into the sea, and the waters roar.[15] It is through the practice of contemplation that we learn to see God all around us and we are drawn to worship Him. It is through this reflection that we seek His face and receive in turn the image of who we are in Him. Focusing on the Presence of God within absorbs the sacred into our thinking and perceiving. The spring of living water that Jesus talks about in John 4: 14 wells up within us and drenches the thirsty, arid parts of our being. We don't make it happen because it's already at work, we just give our attention to it and become what we behold. The best thing we can do is let it flow without impediment. This is difficult when we are used to being in charge. It's hard to learn that God's action does not rely on us. It is a sign of His blessing and generosity that He gives to His children. It is not our responsibility. Rohr writes:

'You are in a position of total powerlessness, and your ego is fighting it. All you can do is surrender and enter into this dance of unhindered dialogue, this circle of praise, this web of communion that we call the Blessed Trinity.' [16]

This brings another knotty problem to the surface. The challenge of our own egos and the discomfort of feeling vulnerable. We defend ourselves against anything we fear will lessen our control and dilute our independence. We may cover it over by purposeful action because it is when we are doing something – anything- we are filling the void within us. The hole needs to be stuffed to ensure that we don't feel the discomfort it brings, reminding us that we are not as self-sufficient as we thought. We war against the idea of surrender because we imagine it is the place of failure and weakness. It is the white flag of shame. We have been found wanting and it is humiliating. But this cannot be seen in this way when we know who it is that we are submitting to. God is not a tyrant oppressing us until we give in. He is a loving Father drawing us into His embrace and kissing us when we are dirty, dishevelled and smell of pigswill.

Surrender comes more easily when we focus on who God is, not what we've made Him to be. If Jesus is the image and perfect blueprint for God,[17] then we look through the Son's character to illuminate the Father. Just like the disciple Philip, we are to recognise that Jesus shows us what the Father is like.[18] When we look at Jesus, we need to look nowhere else.

Gordian Knots imply the need for decisive, bold action. There is no gentle teasing out or unravelling. There is a swift response that invites a paradigm shift in perception. We slice through that which has kept us bound with the sword of truth, whether it's concepts of the conditional love of God, a faulty image of ourselves, or a fear of vulnerability and abuse that keeps us from surrender. These things cannot co-habit with the truth of who God is, who He says we are, and how He loves us. They need to be removed. What grows in their place is the focus on God that leads to the experience *of* God. It is the sacred space that is then filled with His presence. It is a maturing into simplicity, not a distraction into confusion and complexity.

When I reflect on my faith journey, I can see how easy it is to be distracted. Whenever my focus is on me and how I can make my way towards God, I am bound up with my performance. How am I doing in my disciplines, rituals, devotional life, and church attendance? I monitor my attempts to get closer to Him and ultimately, my shortcomings and failures. I concentrate on conforming to what I think God wants me to be and do.

When I was a child I was not in the habit of going to church, therefore when I started to go, I had to get used to a different culture. I worked to fit in with my fellow Christians and learned what it meant to be part of a local church with all its practices, traditions and cultural expectations. I even attempted on several occasions to keep a swear-box. I would put money in it every time I uttered one of my 'earthy phrases'. The money would be donated to charity and over time, it was my hope that I would learn to curb my language. I never succeeded in my goal, although the charities benefitted significantly.

However hard I prayed, read chunks of the Bible, or went to church, there was always a subtle sense of disappointment. I wasn't where I wanted to be, where I thought others were, and the concept of holiness seemed completely alien to me. If I did have periods of time when I was demonstrating some discipline at last, I couldn't sustain it. At least my failure made any smugness short-lived. These distractions continued as I devoured books and went on courses to explore whatever was the hot Christian topic of the time. There was so much activity but little movement towards maturity.

None of this was wrong or undesirable, but I couldn't help wondering whether there was something missing. I had experienced the power of the Holy Spirit, and even had knowledge and practice of some of the spiritual gifts, but still I was left pondering about *the more*. This intensified after my recent reading of the cultural context behind the parable of the two lost sons and the compassionate father. As I pondered this familiar story with a new lens, I realised that I was essentially looking down the wrong end of the telescope. I came to the conclusion this isn't about me; this is always about the nature of God. This is always about who He is, what He thinks of us, and how He behaves towards us. It is fine to practice my spiritual devotions and disciplines, but I don't need to find a way to God because I am there with Him already. God has found me. He has made up the distance and all I need to do is to accept being found.

This was another sea-change and one that brought massive relief. The truth is I am living *from* union with God, not *for* it. I realised much of my angst about getting closer to God has been self-generated from a place of my own insecurity. It isn't real. It is a distraction, and it is something that doesn't come from God. I have expended lots of wasted energy into feeling that I need to do more or be more, when God-with-us is the only *more* I need.

This underlines the required shift in my thinking, switching my focus off my performance as a disciple and onto God's love, grace, and mercy. This isn't a licence to behave as I want as I still intend to honour God, but this is out of gratitude not servitude. I can experience the beautiful benefit of being primarily God's friend rather than His servant.[19] As we magnify the Lord, we acknowledge Him in all His greatness and His tender mercy, and this isn't an excuse to move on to castigate ourselves as worthless sinners. I'm not sure that berating ourselves over our wrongdoing helps anyone to get closer to God; it just teaches people to hate themselves and others. To allow the conviction of the Holy Spirit, to confess and be forgiven, however, is another thing entirely. Again, we do so *from* our friendship with God, not in a quest *for* it.

I want to end this chapter with two short stories which connect with the quotation from Thomas Merton at the beginning of the chapter about the decluttering of our lives. One is from Blake Healy's book, *Indestructible*. Blake had left his children's paddling pool out for several days. He planned to empty it, but he didn't get round to it. When he eventually went to do it, he saw that it was full of mosquito larvae. He dumped most of it out on the grass and in a fit of disgust he poured bleach into the remaining water in the pool. Then he realised that he didn't want to pour the bleach out onto the grass, so he had to prevent the children from using the pool for a while. Each day he found reasons not to address the problem but when he eventually did, he was shocked to find that the bleach chemicals had evaporated over time and now the pool was once again full of mosquito larvae. The point he makes is that if we want transformation, we must change our environment for good. Short term solutions are not the answer. A complete shift in thinking is needed.

The second short story I have is from our family. Neither my husband nor I are hoarders, but I tolerate a lot more clutter than Patrick does. Every now and then he feels the need to purge what we have in the house. A skip will arrive on the driveway, and he will merrily fill it with all the things that no longer work or have outlived their usefulness. He makes space by being ruthless about things we no longer use or look at. Where I might be tempted to keep something, 'just in case we may need it again,' for him - it's straight into the skip.

We all benefit from this kind of industrial spring clean, not only of the 'stuff' that is in our houses, but the things that we carry that clutter up our mental and emotional space. This might be a distorted identity of who we are, or anxiety over whether we are good enough for God, or whether our performance gets us closer to Him. The truth is we are who God says we are; He is the One who makes us worthy; and we are already found by Him. Nothing we can do or say could make Him love us less. When we know the Truth, it will set us free and it will highlight all the things that we hold onto that are now redundant. One helpful analogy that is common to many of us, is the warnings we get that we are using up space on our computer. I regularly have to purge my storage space, getting rid of duplicate files or film clips that use up masses of space on my hard-drive. When I get rid of things that I don't need any more I find my computer works better and faster. It is streamlined and better able to deal with the tasks I have it for. How much better our life functions when we can get rid of the 'stuff' we have discovered we no longer need.

This process and the stories I've just told, remind us that at times the gentle, little by little approach doesn't work. We need a seismic shift in our thinking that allows us to dump the junk we've all become accustomed to and mistakenly believe we need. These thoughts and practices are not inherently bad, but they distract us. They keep up from our freedom. They keep us looking at ourselves and others: comparing, contrasting, and competing. We become the subject of working out our own salvation, not the object of God's invincible love.

The course correction required means replacing the old with transformed thinking for a new season. This can't be unravelled and teased out because this is like the Gordian knot.

Sometimes you just need to pick up the sword of truth and slice through it to be free.

11

THE QUESTION OF POWER

The heroes of the upside-down kingdom are not warrior kings riding in chariots or peasant kings carrying pitchforks. The heroes of his kingdom are children and servants. These lowly ones carry the new flag of the servant regime. They operate not by the power of might and force but by the sustaining power of the Holy Spirit flowing from the mountain of God.'

Donald B. Kraybill

'Part of the journey towards healing is about discovering the character of God through the lens of Jesus, learning that He is completely trustworthy and utterly loving. We will only let our defences down when we know that the One to whom we entrust ourselves is safe to be with and won't destroy us in our submission.'

The Ambassador

Lord Acton famously said, *'Power tends to corrupt and absolute power corrupts absolutely.'* [1] Although this is a popular quotation it is a sweeping statement by itself. Power is not a single thing. It may take many forms such as political, military, economic, social, or religious. There is also 'soft power.' Joseph Nye of Harvard University coined this term in the 1990's, to describe the ability to co-opt, rather than coerce. This has been expressed recently by the arrival of a growing breed of 'influencers,' whose popularity on social media platforms motivates their followers to buy products that are endorsed on their channel. This is power, but can we talk about it in the same way as, for example, political power? If not, does that mean that there are some kinds of power we may exercise without being colonised by potential negative effects? Or does all power, by its nature, become seductive and morally corrosive? Is it the thin end of the wedge? A gateway activity that hooks our egos into a sense of self-importance, inflated agency, and a need to control? The subject of power is both confusing and controversial, but it is a vital issue to engage with as we consider the role of an ambassador.

First, it's helpful to look more closely at what Jesus says in the gospels about the power dynamics of the kingdom of God. As the quotation at the beginning of the chapter illustrates, power looks different in the kingdom. Kraybill states:

'Jesus redefined the meaning of power when he refused to use violent force...Matthew and Mark report three occasions when Jesus spoke of suffering as the new form of messianic power. Each time the disciples were arguing over how much power and authority they would have in the kingdom. In all three cases, Jesus responded by teaching them about suffering discipleship.' [2]

This suffering love would fit with the image described in Philippians chapter two, saying that Jesus: -

'who, being in very nature God,
did not consider equality with God something to be used to his own advantage;
rather he made himself nothing by taking the very nature of a servant,
being made in human likeness.
And being found in appearance as a man,
he humbled himself by becoming obedient to death –
even death on a cross! [3]

This definition of power is uncomfortable because it goes against the grain of human nature. It doesn't make sense to us that there is power in suffering, but this is something Jesus is clear about. He illustrated this on the eve of the crucifixion when He commands His disciples to love one another as He has loved them. He shows this by acting as a servant in washing their feet before the meal. Then

He takes the bread and wine of the Passover meal and makes it the symbol and sacrament of the breaking of His body and the pouring out of His blood.[4] These actions show that Jesus is getting ready to lay down His life, as He has previously said He would willingly do.[5] This laying down however, does not mean that He is emptied of all power and the forces of darkness have won. He corrects this assumption by saying to the disciples:

'I will no longer talk much with you, for the ruler of this world is coming. He has no power over me;' [6]

The disciples would have been confused about this when they see Jesus crucified the next day. From a worldly perspective, any power He has is crushed by the occupying regime who execute Him. His followers do not rescue Him, and there is no popular uprising in support. He shares the same fate as many revolutionaries at the time, because Rome is not known for its leniency. But because we know this is not the end of the story, we read back into His comment that power can take different forms.

C. S. Lewis writes about this different perspective in his children's book *The Lion, The Witch and The Wardrobe*. After the great Lion, Aslan, had been shaved, tied up and killed, the Witch and her co-conspirators rejoice and believe that they have won and Aslan's power has gone for good. Lucy and Susan keep the body of Aslan company, but in the cold morning air they begin to walk back and forth to keep themselves warm. It is while they are away from the corpse that they hear a deafening crack. Running back to where the sound came from, they see the stone table, on which Aslan was killed, has been broken in two. They cannot see Aslan's body anywhere and fear it has been taken away. Then they see Aslan himself, fully alive again, shining in the sunrise, larger than they had seen him before, shaking his mane. In the conversation that follows Aslan explains what has happened.

"It means" said Aslan, "that though the Witch knew the Deep Magic, there is a magic deeper still which she did not know. Her knowledge goes back only to the dawn of time. But if she could have looked a little further back, into the stillness and the darkness before Time dawned, she would have read there a different incantation. She would have known that when a willing victim who had committed no treachery was killed in a traitor's stead, the Table would crack and Death itself would start working backwards.' [7]

We are unlikely to call God's power 'magic' but this story does point to a way of looking at this subject. It's the power of *undoing*. The Passion Translation of 1 John 3: 8 states:

'The reason the Son of God was revealed was to undo and destroy the works of the devil.'

This means reversing the works of darkness but not by using the same weapons that accomplished that evil in the first place. Jesus advocates a different way, which is why He commands the disciples to put their swords away when He is arrested in Gethsemane.[8] Matthew's gospel adds further explanation with:

'for all who draw the sword will die by the sword. Do you think I cannot call on my Father, and he will at once put at my disposal more than twelve legions of angels? But how then would the Scriptures be fulfilled that say it must happen in this way?' [9]

There is power in heaven available to the Son, but He chooses not to use it because of the purposes of God. What we see in the ministry of Jesus is the refusal to use physical force as a weapon. He stands against the prevailing culture and the myth of redemptive violence which proposes that our own violent response to invading forces is 'redeemed' because it rids our society of the evil that was taking hold. In addition, this belief system employs projection and scapegoating to ensure that all wickedness is located outside of ourselves, making our enemies thoroughly bad, and us, thoroughly righteous, even though we may retaliate in the same violent ways as them. Walter Wink states:

'The myth of redemptive violence is nationalism become absolute. This myth speaks for God; it does not listen for God to speak. It invokes the sovereignty of God as its own...It misappropriates the language, symbols, and scriptures of Christianity. Its offer is not forgiveness

but victory...It is idolatrous. And it is immensely popular.'[10]

Wink's argument is very challenging because it reveals the prevailing attitude in times of conflict, common among the nations. We can see how wrapping a foreign policy decision in the flag makes it more difficult to oppose. To stand against it is unpopular and critics appear unpatriotic and weak-willed or cowardly. Taking seriously how Jesus resists armed conflict creates a problem when the State looks for the approval and support of the Church for the agreement of a 'just war'. Wink clarifies that Jesus teaches nonviolence, not 'just war.' As Gandhi observed, *"The only people on earth who do not see Christ and His teaching as nonviolent are Christians."*[11]

Jesus, however, does not expect passivity in the face of evil. He advocates a third way, which is non-violent resistance. It is about attacking accusers with the truth, sometimes verbally, sometimes in action. Read within the context of non-violent resistance, walking the extra mile, turning the other cheek, and giving the coat and shirt to those who demand it, are not about passive submission. They are all about subverting power and shifting it away from the dominator, recalling them to their own humanity and to the humanity of their victim.[12]

This third way has often been expressed in situations which could have easily escalated into bloodshed. It is particularly effective when surprise at a creative response interrupts the plan for violence. When the Hispanic Council of Belsenville, Illinois, discovered that the Ku Klux Klan was planning a rally at the county courthouse, they decided to protest the Klan's racism by serenading the KKK with a thirteen-piece mariachi band. It then became a festival of Latino culture.[13] Another story involves a man being met by an armed thief as he came out of a bus station. Instead of responding naturally with fear or anger, the man showed concern saying *"It's cold. Why don't you take my jacket?"*. The gunman was confused, so the man continued in a natural manner, *"I was just going for something to eat. Why don't you join me?"* He even offered some money, which the gunman refused.[14]

Creative sentencing can help learning rather than perpetuate abusive cycles that can often escalate into violence. This happened in the case where a slum landlord, up before a judge for housing-code violations, was sentenced to live for one month in one of his own rat-infested rooms with broken pipes and no heat. It also happened after some young vandals had defaced the walls of a synagogue with graffiti, including swastikas. The rabbi intervened with the judge, and it was agreed that they young people had to spend thirty hours studying Judaism with the rabbi, growing respect for the Jewish faith and the rabbi himself.[15]

Another attack against a Jewish family in Montana came when a neo-Nazi hate group threw a block at a child's bedroom window because he had a menorah on show for Chanukah. As a sign of solidarity with the family, the local church congregation hung pictures of menorahs in their windows. The idea spread and more and more people who wanted to support their Jewish neighbours did the same. There were neo-Nazi attacks, but the community refused to back down.[16] Diffusing aggression and violence by solidarity is a common thread, as well as offering hospitality. In the UK, members of the English Defence League gathered to protest at an Islamic Centre in York. The Centre then opened its doors and invited the protestors in for tea and biscuits and even an impromptu game of football.[17]

The history of non-violence involves boycotts and demonstrations. Rosa Parks famously refused to give up her seat to a white man in Alabama, 1955, sparking the Montgomery bus boycotts which are part of the civil rights struggle in America. There have been many examples of non-violent resistance that highlight an evil without perpetuating violence, but that is not to say that bloodshed is not involved. It can be a costly experience for those who remain committed to its ideals, producing martyrs for the cause as illustrated by Martin Luther King and Gandhi.

When we look at the life of Jesus, we can see

that, unlike the zealots of His day, He does not urge armed conflict against the oppression of Rome, but He still exercises an extraordinary amount of power. It is just a different kind to what the world knows. We see His miracles of salvation, healing, deliverance, and resurrection. We see His power over the elements and nature as He calms storms, walks on the water, and curses the fig-tree. We see Him changing water to wine and multiplying sources of food. After He is risen from the dead, we see Him coming through locked doors, appearing and disappearing at will, and yet still having a corporeal existence that allows Him to eat a fish breakfast with His friends. This power does not end with His Ascension either. At Pentecost, we see the outpouring of the Holy Spirit on all the disciples and now they too can bring healing, deliverance, and new life to the dead in Jesus' name. The book of Acts is the unfolding story of a church transformed by the empowering Spirit of God within. The Apostle Paul writes:

'My message and my preaching were not with wise and persuasive words, but with a demonstration of the Spirit's power, so that your faith might not rest on human wisdom, but on God's power.' [18]

This is the point. It is not human power in terms of military or political might, or even soft power and influence. This power is from the Holy Spirit and it comes from God, not us. Although there are some who believe that all miracles ceased after the age of the Apostles, church history begs to differ and there are signs and wonders recorded in every century since.

Our minds are a constant battleground over what we believe and what we seek after. When we engage with the subject of power there are questions that arise. Is God's power available to us in the same ways as it was to the first disciples? And, bearing in mind power's potentially corrosive effect, should we be seeking it out anyway? We might also want to consider what makes God's power within us different from religious power viewed from a worldly perspective. There is no doubt that religion has power. Critics of faith love to argue how religion often provides a motivation for war, even if what is adhered to and promoted is a warped reflection, bearing little resemblance to its true spirit. This distortion becomes the new vision of the old truth. It drifts from the original intention and becomes an explanation and justification of humanity's desires. When religion is used in this way it mutates into being culture's servant and defender, rather than its prophet and judge. Some may argue that this is enough to ensure that we don't seek power. We cannot trust ourselves with it and, looking at the history books, there is plenty of evidence for this thinking.

This is where the story of Jesus laying down His power becomes an expression of our faith. We argue that Jesus didn't seek power, and therefore we shouldn't either. We propose that we most resemble Jesus when we let go of all our control and influence and become *power-less.* Is this what God wants for us? Opinion is divided. In his book *Going Empty-Handed* Ian Cowley writes:

'The Holy Spirit sometimes leads us also, like Jesus, into the place of weakness, of lostness, of emptiness, where we have to cry out to God to help us and to save us. The wonderful truth which the Bible shows us is that God is there in the desert with us, and with him the desert becomes a place of deep and lasting spiritual growth and empowering. Often we will come to see that the things which God has taught us in the desert are things which we could not have learnt anywhere else.' [19]

This is spiritual wisdom. There are some things we cannot learn until we are at the end of ourselves. We allow God's strength in our weakness, recognising that we do not have the resources within to fix ourselves or our world. Thomas a Kempis wrote in the fifteenth century:

'Be not angry that you cannot make others as you wish them to be, since you cannot make yourself as you wish to be.' [20]

Recognising our lack of power may be an honest reflection of our true state, but facing it every day and living within it, feels uncomfortable. It can be dangerous too. It increases our probability of being taken advantage of by others, being bullied, abused, silenced, and ignored. If we have worldly power, at least we can stand up for ourselves, be believed when reporting offences to the authorities, and be able to act in response. Bullies and abusers tend not to pick on those who can inflict damage in return. They target the weak, the dependent, and the power-less, trusting that their actions will not be revisited on them.

It is not surprising that those who have been abused find the idea of trusting God difficult. The concept of Him being all-powerful and yet totally good is hard to grasp when we have experienced power that has been misused and brought evil into our lives. Part of the journey towards healing is about discovering the character of God through the lens of Jesus, learning that He is completely trust-worthy and utterly loving. We will only let our defences down when we know that the One to whom we entrust ourselves is safe to be with and won't destroy us in our submission. This is some-thing to keep in mind when those of us who have not experienced the misuse of power preach the need to lay ourselves down to those of us who have.

It is also important to recognise that the language of power is significant, and we must learn from others what it means to them. For example, 98% of adults prosecuted for sexual offences are men.[21] When we exclusively talk about God as He and Him, and Father, and refer to all members of the

Godhead as male, the Church can be seen as an androcratic system. It can become a barrier in the way for those among us who have been abused by male power.

Power is not politically neutral and value-free. It is a journey of revelation for all of us to discover and understand what it means to the oppressed and how interpreting scripture in particular ways feeds into this. This is not about political correctness. This is about being sensitive to the humanity in one another and being humble enough to learn, recognising that privilege does exist, as does prejudice, and experiences of power may vary widely depending on who is telling their story.

For some, the idea of seeking God's power is a thinly-veiled reframing of a desire for worldly power. We want to feel successful and effective, so we just swap our focus to a more acceptable faith-based power. This is a minefield but one we must navigate if we are to understand the relationship there is between our faith, God's power, and earthly power. This makes the question multi-dimensional. It is not straight forward. Neither is it a question that can be answered by saying that it is 'all' about emptying ourselves of power, or 'all' about stepping up into God's power. In considering the role of an ambassador we see the coming together of both. An ambassador is not powerful in themselves, but they are powerful because of who they represent. We also see that expressed by our God-given identity. It is knowing who we are *in Him* as a son or daughter, that enables us to live from a place of fullness not emptiness.

When we talk about power from God it's important to qualify it. This is not about dominating or riding roughshod over others or thinking we can work in the strength of our own resources. The writer and pastor, Danny Silk, states:

'Powerful people take responsibility for their lives and choices...choose who they want to be with, what they are going to pursue in life, and how they are going to go after it...Powerful people do not try to control other people. They know it doesn't work, and that it's not their job. Their job is to control themselves...They don't try to get people to respect them; they create a respectful environment by showing respect. They deliberately set the standard for how they expect to be treated by the way they treat others.' [22]

As an ambassador, we are not filled with ourselves and our own ego and desires. We are representatives of the king and that carries with it a dignity of office as we and others respond to the delegated authority that we carry. This confers a sense of power and to hide from this in the fear that we will lose ourselves to pride and self-importance is missing the point. Any power is given, not earned, and perhaps this is where the nuance applies to going to God empty-handed. We invite God to fill us with His identity and influence so we can fulfil the role of an ambassador in the world for Him. This is power that is rooted in the relationship we have with the Godhead and not to live and move within it is to misrepresent our king. Power, therefore, despite its many dangers and pitfalls, is an essential part of our calling but only when it expresses kingdom values and the love and purposes of our king.

12

COMMUNICATION WITH HQ

*'I*t's about learning who God is, learning who you are, and learning how to see through the eyes of love.'

Shawn Bolz

'All of this is an ongoing, life-long, process. There are always new things to learn but we can begin to discern more clearly with practice. What we must remember is that God longs to communicate with His children and He will help us every step of the way.'

The Ambassador

One of the roles of an ambassador is keeping in contact with officials from their own country so that their homeland's view can be expressed reliably. In times past this was done through letters that were often coded as there was a danger in correspondence being intercepted by spies. In the political realm there are great advantages in knowing how one country will respond to the actions of another or what a government may be planning, especially in times of conflict. Sir Francis Bacon, the sixteenth century British Statesman, may have been accredited with the phrase *'Knowledge is Power'* but its roots go back to the book of Proverbs in the Hebrew Scriptures.[1]

When we consider being Christ's ambassadors there is no need for secrecy but there is an absolute requirement to ensure that we communicate with Headquarters. The added challenge is that God does not send letters, emails, texts, or make phone calls. His communication is by a myriad of means but we must be the ones to decode it.

One major way God speaks is through the Bible, and I'm not just talking about gaining the wisdom through stories of what happened to others. God has a way of bringing ancient scripture to our attention and letting it speak into our modern lives. Word and Spirit work together in this process and it's common for people to say things like *'that sentence just stood out for me,'* or *'that phrase flew off the page at me.'* It is the receptor within that takes the written word and sees how it points to the Living Word of God, who is Jesus. The Bible isn't a dead text that we prod and dissect to understand, much like we would if we were performing an autopsy on a corpse. It is living and therefore there is a two-way relationship here. While we may assume that studying the Bible is all about us judging and interpreting the text, we discover that it returns the favour and, at times, its teeth can bite. Hebrews 4: 12 states:

'For the word of God is alive and active. Sharper than any double-edged sword, it penetrates even to dividing soul and spirit, joints and marrow; it judges the thoughts and attitudes of the heart.'

Therefore, if we want to hear from God, a good place to start is with what He has already said in the Bible. Then as we read *with* God, the wind of the Spirit blows on the words causing sparks to catch fire. Suddenly we are ablaze with revelation through the Spirit of Truth within us. This is vital for an ambassador, and anyone who wishes to be a good one will recognise that learning about the heart of the sovereign and the values of the kingdom is essential.

Some of us may treat the idea of 'new learning' with suspicion. We fear that looking at the Bible with fresh eyes may distort or corrupt it. We may hold fast to the warning in 2 Timothy 4: 3 that there will come a time when people will not put up with sound doctrine but will gather around those who say what they want to hear. Our uncompromising stance therefore becomes a sign of being faithful to *the true Gospel* and any new scholarship, cultural explanation or linguistical clarification is to be resisted. When we assume that there is nothing new to learn and that the interpretation we have received is the only accurate one, scripture is put in a straight-jacket. It says more about our need to be right than it does about the texts themselves.

Over the centuries there has been much division and blood shed due to the rigidity of how scripture has been taught and handed down to us. We can miss the point that all interpretation is subject to our social, geographical and historical context. Even the translations that we use put a different emphasis on meaning and particular words. As Kenneth Bailey writes:

'Translation is always commentary. The translators must try to understand the text, and only then can they present it in the receptor language.' [2]

This was illustrated when translators for the Revised Standard Version (RSV) were studying Romans 16: 7. Paul was sending greetings to Adronicus and Junia who he had been imprisoned with. He says that they are 'outstanding among the apostles.' This posed a problem for the translators because Junia was clearly a feminine proper name. They were unable, or unwilling, to believe that there were women apostles and therefore they assumed that Paul must have been speaking about a man.

They therefore added an 's' to Junia, making it a male name. In the RSV it then read;

*'Greet Andronicus and Junias my kins**men** and my fellow prisoners; they are **men** of note among the apostles.'* [3]

This was corrected in the new version, (the NRSV translation) but it proves that to translate means to interpret and we cannot always see that our cultural biases play a part in this.

Letting scripture breathe in us is about entering into this life-long experience of learning. I continue to be fascinated by the cultural background to the gospels and by understanding more of Jesus' Jewish heritage. Without that richness to contribute to my learning, I am at risk of importing my Eurocentric view on what is going on in each of the stories. I would also be in more danger of using certain verses that support my cultural reading of the text, while ignoring others that may give a different stance or meaning.

Lesslie Newbigin, who was a theologian and bishop of the Church of South India, stated that our reason is profoundly shaped by our culture and tradition; it does not operate in a vacuum. We therefore use cultural lenses when we come to read the Bible. We might understand the primary intent of the story, but all the inner nuances will be out of focus, with the consequence that some of the deeper meaning, humour, and tensions will be blurred, if not missed altogether. His remedy for this is to study the Bible with others whose minds have been shaped by other cultures.[4] It is through that engagement that we discover how our thoughts and beliefs have become 'syncretistic', that is, a blend of different models of thought from religious and secular sources. Newbigin discovered that what he had taken for granted as 'a proper reading of the text' was, in fact, shaped by his intellectual formation in the modern scientific worldview. His Christianity was an amalgamation but so was the interpretation of his Indian companions. This puts space between us and the original context of the words and, because we don't always see our own lenses, it can bias, and therefore distort, our understanding.

One example Kenneth Bailey gives is a translation of Matthew 5: 14-15, where Jesus is speaking about the light of the world and saying, 'Nor do *they* light a lamp.' The original RSV translated the phrase 'nor do *men* light a lamp' but those in the culture Jesus was speaking to knew that it was *women* who had this role. Bailey reminds us that this kind of cultural fine tuning is a vital component of the task of interpretation.[5]

This small example is significant when we are talking about inclusion. If the default viewpoint is seeing men as the actors within a given context, who are seen and heard and have power and presence, what are the women doing? If they are erased from the scene, how can their role as full partners be normalised? Caroline Criado Perez sums it up by saying:

'...men go without saying, and women don't get said at all. Because when we say human, on the whole, we mean man.' [6]

This has been encouraged by our use of language which still absorbs women into the terms of *Man, Men,* and *Mankind* . When women are not being seen as distinct from men, there can be cultural assumptions that they are not there. This perpetuates the cycle of prejudice as illustrated by the previous example of Junia the Apostle. Without critical analysis of what we bring to our reading of the Bible, we may leap from reasoning that if women *weren't* there as leaders and apostles, then women *shouldn't* be in that role now. Sadly, this patriarchal bias has in some places prevented the full contribution women have to offer and the whole Body of Christ is the poorer for it.

Respecting and honouring scripture therefore requires us to become aware of our lenses. This is not about pushing a political agenda, this is about being modest enough to recognise that we haven't got the full picture and there is always more to learn. If we fail to take this challenge seriously, we run the risk of distorting Scripture, perpetuating poor practices in our churches and harming others. The

Church is only just beginning to understand the damage inflicted by spiritual abuse and where, among other behaviours, scripture is weaponised to coercively control others. Speaking out provokes resistance and rejection from the majority. One way to counter such unhealthy dynamics is to ensure that space and permission is given to allow for difference without censorship. Dr Lisa Oakley and Justin Humphreys write in their book *Escaping the Maze of Spiritual Abuse;*

'..it matters how we treat people who disagree with us. If we pressure people into agreeing with our viewpoint we steer away from the freedom God gives us to choose' [7]

New learning does not immediately assume a more liberal viewpoint. We are all learners together and recognise that our fellow Christians from around the world may interpret the Bible very differently from us. I remember hearing someone say that, *'the only difference between Fundamentalists and Liberals is what they are fundamentalist about.'* Expressing humility is essential and, although we treat the Bible with the utmost respect, we do not worship it as an idol. Instead, we sit at the feet of Jesus of Nazareth. He is the Living Word to which our sacred texts point. To interpret them without the aid of God's Holy Spirit is to miss their heart. Communication as an ambassador therefore requires a connection with the author, not just the correspondence itself.

When I started considering the other ways that God communicates, I immediately felt that I wasn't qualified to write about it. I felt that I should do what I always do and read a book by someone whom I considered knew much more about the subject than me. This prompted a friend of mine to challenge me. She invited me to write what I already knew about. The result was a series of ten short podcasts on *'Hearing from God: A Beginner's Guide.'* [8] This illustrated what is true for most of us: we can be quick to believe we are not qualified to talk about a particular subject when in fact God has already made us so through His indwelling Spirit. We have all we need to make a start but confidence is only built through practice. Writing and recording the series of podcasts proved to me that I already had lots of knowledge, from the Scriptures themselves and from receiving the teaching of others. I also had my own experience.

One of the biggest hurdles we face is allowing ourselves to believe that God speaks to *us*, not just to those we consider more worthy or spiritual. One way to combat this is to face our anxieties head on and take some risks. If we see ourselves as a student learning about the ways God communicates, it takes the pressure off us from having to become an expert overnight. Mistakes are a natural part of the learning process and God understands this.

It is like watching a child's progress in learning to walk. First, an infant starts to roll on his or her side, then they begin sitting up; this is followed by bottom shuffling, and then crawling. The child then starts to pull him or herself up and holds onto furniture, and then the fun really begins when the child takes those first few steps. Even when a child falls again, it doesn't matter, because they are on their way and with every small success they grow in confidence, muscle memory, and proficiency. Just as we would be cheering our child along for every step, even with a few bumps along the way, I believe that God cheers us on as we step out in faith.

This was certainly my starting point when I began to learn to give prophetic encouragement to others. By this I mean attempting to hear specific words from God for a particular person. It involves encouraging that person that they are known and loved by God and He is interested in all aspects of their life. We are told to:

'Follow the way of love and eagerly desire gifts of the Spirit, especially prophecy.' [9]

This, however, is not something that is spoken much about or encouraged outside of the Pentecostal/Renewal wings of the Church. This may be because the practice of prophecy connects us with the concept of prophets. This evokes images of strange, wild-eyed hermits proclaiming judgement on people with a thumping 'Thus Saith The Lord' attached to it. In the absence of corrective experiences, our anxieties firmly shut the door on John the Baptist stereotypes turning up and causing havoc in our well-ordered churches.

An ambassador, however, wants to ensure that every opportunity is given to express the Sovereign's word to people, whether they see themselves as citizens of heaven or not. Shawn Bolz says it like this:

'You are translating the culture of heaven and the heart of the Father. If you want to grow, get to know his heart culture. Look at all the ways he is talking to you.' [10]

My previous book, and much of the earlier chapters of this book, have been about getting rid of some of the emotional baggage and distortions about God I carried. Through it, I feel that I have been learning more about His nature and who He is. This has become an encouragement to me because I have realised how many of my more recent gains in revelation have led to greater freedom and self-acceptance. I can now detect and erode patterns of negative thinking that drag me down and I feel lighter in my Spirit as I discover more about the Holy Trinity and enjoy greater intimacy.

To ensure that I remain on the right path, I've been encouraged to create a communication superhighway with Him. I felt that God was telling me that the more I came back to Him to pray and to listen, the more it would become a pattern. It would then become a well-beaten track, then a path, then a road, then a motorway. This was about building a connection that was so well-used to constant traffic both ways that the communication superhighway would be established. This is what a good ambassador needs. I therefore pursued listening to God with greater intensity.

I have already had some experience of sharing words of prophetic encouragement with others. I don't want to force words on people who don't welcome them, so I always give the opportunity for people to act as their own gatekeepers. I listen to God and write down some encouragement that I feel God is saying to them. I then tell them they are to judge the word themselves to see if it resonates with them. I tell them I am learning to hear from God and therefore if some parts of what I have written don't hit the mark, that is okay. This is an experimental process for me and they are at liberty to let anything that doesn't feel right to 'fall to the ground.' However, if there are things that really make an impact, it would be good to hear. All feedback is welcome so I can learn from it.

Over a number of years of practice I have been staggered by the response. Many times people are moved to tears because the words speak to a need or a situation that I have known nothing about. They feel affirmed and loved by God. Even when there isn't a sense of resonance, sometimes this comes later, even years later, and the person excitedly comes back to tell me. The process of writing prophetic encouragement is like taking hold of the top of a tissue in a box. I can only see a fraction of it when I start to write, but as I continue and get into the flow, it is like pulling on the tissue and more and more material comes into my hand. This experience helps me not to panic when I can't discern anything at first. God is well able to provide. Receiving feed-back encourages me hugely, especially when it is right on target in a way I couldn't have known before.

I have been collecting stories and written responses about the words I give. God is so gracious to me giving me encouragement through it, perhaps by first directing me to the low-hanging fruit. As I have practised, however, I've learned more about the listening process. It is a thrilling adventure.

After a number of years sharing prophetic words with those I knew would be open to it, (or at least not terrified by it), I have become bolder. I have begun to evaluate what it feels like to write from the heart of God, to discern the *weight* a particular word may have and to see if, when, and how, it hits the mark. I received some online mentoring via a course by Shawn Bolz who teaches extensively about prophecy. In terms of the learning experience he writes:

'My mentor used to say, "if my prophecy is right, then bless you! If it is wrong, then bless me for trying. Either way both, or one of us, are blessed." She always said this to help people overcome rejection and fear when trying to prophesy.' [11]

I am always willing to invite the Body of Christ to scrutinise and weigh up any word I give. I recognise that discernment is an important part of the process. I always say "If I don't take the risk to be wrong, I can never be right either" and that helps me to ensure humility and accountability in the process.

Building the communication superhighway has also involved the practice of two-way journaling. I heard a podcast from Mark Virkler about this process and, as someone who has kept a journal for over thirty years, I felt it was something that I could relate to. This practice is not about learning from an academic source. It isn't even about a formal technique as such. This is much more about being open and intuitive to the Holy Spirit within, with a few preliminaries to help with the flow.

Virkler explains four keys to hearing God's voice. The first is recognising that God's voice exists as spontaneous thoughts which come into our minds. The second requires us to quieten ourselves so we can listen. The third key, he describes as 'look for vision as you pray.'[12] He expands this by suggesting that we notice the flow of thoughts and pictures that come to us, opening our logical and visionary faculties for the Holy Spirit to use, with the results that we experience Spirit led reasoning and godly imagination, visions and dreams. The last key is to write down the flow of thoughts and pictures that come to us. He summarises these keys as stillness, vision, spontaneity and journaling.[13]

Following this pattern, I began by opening a spiral bound notebook, finding a quiet space and beginning to write a question to God. Then I waited – ensuring I was relaxed but attentive to listen to the voice within. Without stopping to judge or comment on what I was perceiving, I allowed the flow of thoughts to come and I wrote them down. It is very important not to weigh up the words straight away but just to let them flow. Had I attempted to discern their accuracy I would have effectively turned the tap off to further revelation. James Goll says of this method

'The key to proper interpretation is to ask questions.'[14]

Over the period of a few of months I have filled pages and pages of my notebook, always starting with a question, welcoming the flow of thoughts and then writing them down. I was reminded of Jesus words in John 7: 38:

'Whoever believes in me, as Scripture has said, rivers of living water will flow from within them.'

Sometimes I am surprised by what I have written, or I find it challenging. There is plenty to be encouraged by and there seems to be a wisdom beyond my experience. I have started underlining specific sentences and highlighting important points. I feel I am learning from God's Spirit within and allowing myself to believe that Rhema can indeed shine the light of Truth on my life and lead me into greater revelation and understanding.

I find that I am best at doing this journaling in the morning before the busyness of the day distracts me. Goll writes:

'Stillness is the incubation bed of revelation.'[15]

Having engaged with the discipline of contemplative prayer before, the stillness is not too much of a challenge. I practise being open to the Spirit, and becoming aware through my senses to the presence of God in that moment. I have some coloured pencils by my side and occasionally I draw something. It may be a picture that has come into my mind or something that helps me process what has been said. I know from my parish experience that some people find the idea of drawing something alien and uncomfortable, whereas others find it a natural medium to convey meaning. As a visual processor, I find that images help me think about what I am receiving. They are also a prime way of God communicating, so I take seriously images that pop into my head and dreams I have, bringing them to God in the two-way journaling process.

This experience is so valuable to me that it is not

difficult to continue. I am not always very good at sustaining the practices I take on, but I know I am tapping into a rich vein of revelation in this way and I have the journal to remind me of what's been said. Goll writes:

'Journaling is a fundamental and clearly used biblical tool to help us retain and then properly steward what the Holy Spirit speaks to us.'[16]

It is also building more confidence within; confidence that God is speaking to me and confidence that I can hear Him. It is building the communication superhighway which means that, as an ambassador, I can consult with my king whenever I need to and it is becoming easier over time.

One of the questions that always comes up when we speak about hearing from God is "how do we know that it is really God?" There are no quick and easy answers to this because it is about the process of recognising God's heart, and knowing ourselves. We may have to be particularly discerning in areas where we know we are vulnerable to wanting to hear what we desire. Shawn Bolz has commented on how difficult it is for us to discern accurately words about finding a life's partner or about having children. These areas are so overlaid with emotion and longing that any 'word' must be weighed up very carefully. It is always a good idea in the discernment process to seek wise counsel from others who know and care for us.

All of this is an ongoing, life-long, process. There are always new things to learn but we can begin to discern more clearly with practice. What we must remember is that God longs to communicate with His children and He will help us every step of the way.

13

KINGDOM VALUES

'*Mission has never been a one-way street.*'

Vincent J. Donovan

'It's a simple message, and it starts with us receiving the love of God and allowing that love to be on display. It demonstrates how the power of love made visible in one life, unlocks the Gospel for another.'

The Ambassador

One of the consequences of 'building the bridge as I walk along it' is that I am not working to a schedule or a fully developed plan. This is not like writing a novel or a screenplay where I would have developed the characters and plot and know how the story unfolds in each chapter. In this journey through liminal space, I am required to be open to God's leading and this is not always easy. In my two-way journaling, God has been encouraging me to be more spontaneous with Him, listening for His direction in this moment and obeying Him in the 'now.' It is more immediate and free flowing. Although I am not someone who craves organised schedules, agendas, and strategies to complete them, I do like some structure. God, however, seems to be taking me into a place of being fully present in the moment, attentive, intuitive, and unrehearsed. This came fully into play when I experienced a 'God appointment' in the middle of the night.

I had been writing about kingdom values and had completed about three A4 sides of paper, supported by quotations from various theologians and with biblical references. I had found it hard work but knew it was important to engage with the nuts and bolts of what kingdom life might look like as an ambassador for Christ. The more I read about the parables and all the statements Jesus begins with *'The Kingdom of Heaven/God is like...'* the more complicated it became. I gave myself a break from writing and went to bed.

I had been reading a book by Heidi and Rolland Baker calling *'Learning to love: passion and compassion; the essence of the Gospel.'*[1] I had read several of their books before so I knew it would be simple, inspiring, full of humbling examples of service, and God's miracles breaking though. I wasn't disappointed. After reading for a while, I fell asleep only to wake in the middle of the night with one of their stories going around in my head. The Spirit of God was heavy in the room and I took this as a clear sign that it was time to 'go with it', to pray and open myself up to what God was saying and doing.

The story that sparked this response is retold by Heidi Baker here:

'I was once at a meeting with a very dignified man of God from Germany. He had a beautiful message. When it was my turn to speak, all I had to say through the Holy Spirit was this: "Too big, too small." For about 20 minutes all I felt compelled to say, over and over, was just that: "too big, too small" until the dignified man of God could not stand it any more and would have left if God had not stuck him in his chair. (We are good friends now, by the way!). What did this strange message mean? When your mind is too big and your heart is too small, you can't get anywhere. You can't fly, let alone soar.'

"Truly I tell you, if you have faith as small as a mustard seed, you can say to this mountain, 'Move from here to there,' and it will move. Nothing will be impossible for you." (Matthew 17:20)

Where does the kind of faith that soars come from? It comes from love, from knowing who Jesus is, from understanding what He thinks of you and realizing who He has made you to be. When you are in love you have power. When you start to grasp how wide and long and high and deep is the love of Christ, you start to get full. Full of what? Full of God, full of the understanding that whatever He asks you to do, you can do it; that wherever He asks you to go, you can go. You can live on the edge, because even in the darkest places, light is waiting right there for you. His love, His light in you and I. Passion: it makes us unstoppable.[2]

In that night meeting I felt the conviction that the phrase 'too big, too small' related to me too. While I had attempted to write about what it means to be an ambassador for Christ and had supported my learning with quotations from theologians and respected spiritual writers, I recognised I had lost something, and it was something crucial. Heidi Baker put her finger on it for her German friend and the Holy Spirit did the same for me in the middle of the night.

The mark of all that we are, all that we believe, and all that we do, must be about love. If it's not, then we are not truly representing our kingdom or the king of love. It is God's nature[3] and we cannot be recognised as His, if we do not have an increasing measure of it flowing into our lives. I was writing something that might have had some theological merit and may have interested those within academia but it wasn't about the core value of the kingdom. In my two-way journaling after my night appointment with God, I discerned Him saying:

'I want to expand your heart. It's not about you not using your mind, as I have given you those faculties too, but it is making your heart bigger so it can contain more of My love. This is the most important thing; this is the value that I care about the most.

My love is the measure, so any kingdom value must be led, shaped, and defined by My love. Without that, it is not a 'kingdom value.' Love is the key that opens the door, so ask for more and trust I will give it to you. Do not rely on what you have already. I long to give you more. I long to heal your wounds with My love so that you can carry even more.

Love transforms and lifts up. My love sets you on fire so you burn with compassion and passion for My people. Let My love be the first thing you think about in the morning and the last thing you think about at night. Let it run through and over your day, washing away the anxieties and distractions till only love is left and with that, joy and peace. See your lack and ask for more; there is always more for you.'

God had pushed me to make another course correction on the journey. I was not creating an academic thesis; I was writing for an audience of One. Truth was essential, even if in telling my story I was highlighting my mistakes and back-tracking. Again, in one of my two-way journaling sessions, I heard God saying:

'I want my children to learn the power of acknowl-edging mistakes. I want them to know that I'm not inter-

ested in punishing them, but I want them to learn about Me and themselves. Life involves many course corrections and that's normal. There is power in seeing and re-adjusting your position, staying close, then moving in closer. Encourage others by being real and in writing about My love and My grace. There is always a way back because of what Jesus, My Son, has done for you.'

Love is the key to understanding what it means to be a citizen and ambassador of the kingdom of God. Anything else that sounds good or worthy but does not have love at its root is not part of the king-dom. Love is the measure of all things. Ephesians 3: 16-19 reads:

'I pray that out of his glorious riches he may strengthen you with power through his Spirit in your inner being, so that Christ may dwell in your hearts through faith. And I pray that you being rooted and established in love, may have power, together with all the Lord's holy people, to grasp how wide and long and high and deep is the love of Christ, and to know this love that surpasses knowledge – that you may be filled to the measure of all the fullness of God.'

This is what Heidi Baker was talking about in her story. It's also what her organisation, Iris Global, puts into action when reaching out to communities in the mission field in Mozambique and around the world. She writes:

*'Once they see love, real love from the Master Himself in **our** lives, they come to the King. Entire villages come to*

Jesus when they see that He heals the deaf and blind with just a touch and a word. When we bring a truckload of food for a feast, or solar panel - powered hand - held units that play recordings of the Bible, or new Bibles for the pastors, or clothes, or plastic to rain - proof thatched roofs, the love of God flows freely.' [4]

The Bakers say that 'love must look like something' and therefore there must be a practical outworking that benefits the one who is loved. It is not enough to talk about love and do nothing. If we are to represent the kingdom, love must be at the root of our thinking, speaking, believing, and doing. It's a simple message, and it starts with us receiving the love of God and allowing that love to be on display. It demonstrates how the power of love made visible in one life, unlocks the Gospel for another.

When an ambassador has love on display in his or her life, it can encourage others to want to know more about the kingdom and its king. However, the opposite is also true. Others will make judgements about the kingdom and its values by how its citizens treat people. It is a sad truth that many refuse to show interest in Jesus because of how some of His followers behave. We are advocates for our homeland in both positive and negative ways. We cannot avoid the reality that citizens are seen as reflecting their country.

It's not difficult to find bad press about the Church and at times, it's been encouraged by the very people who have wanted to propagate the Christian message. Vincent Donavan writes:

'Many misgivings, fears, and suspicions revolve around the whole missionary movement and missionary history – the violence done to the cultures, customs, and consciousness of peoples, the callousness and narrow-mindedness found in that history.' [5]

Vincent Donovan was a missionary who left the United States to serve among the Masai in Tanzania. His book, *Christianity Rediscovered* is an extraordinary account of his journey. The legacy of the slave trade and colonial rule survived in local attitudes towards Christianity, and he recognised that what he brought was tied to Western attitudes and assumptions that distracted from a real indigenous discovery of the Gospel. Donovan went through a type of conversion himself as he became critical of previous models of mission and open to what Christianity might look like within the local Masai culture. He became convinced that Salvation history is radically local, and that God is to be found in the cultures of the world, rather than in the Church. Lamin Sanneh, writing about Donovan's legacy states:

'To make headway on the ground, he felt the need to jettison the Western hardware and to begin from the ground up.' [6]

Donovan's cultural baggage was being painfully stripped away through engagement with the Masai and listening and learning from them. In its place, however, a new indigenous expression of Christianity was sprouting up. Lamin Sanneh comments that while Africans reacted to missions as another example of the West's 'unsolicited tutelage', in another way Christianity was offering the language of liberation and equality with which to oppose colonial repression. He writes:

'In reading the Bible in their mother tongue, Africans discovered stories about slavery and liberation, about captivity and restoration, about injustice and vindication and about God's promises to the long-suffering tribes of Isaac and Jacob, and drew appropriate lessons of empowerment from that.'[7]

What this experience shows is that God's truth is relevant to all cultures, in all places, in all times but we must be aware of the clothes in which we dress the message and how this can create barriers that alienate rather than encourage exploration. If we don't want to slow down or distort the message then the 'naked gospel' must come together with the sacred arena of people's lives.[8] Evangelism is therefore less about telling others *our* version of the gospel and more about them discovering the expression of good news *for themselves* which is there already. Vincent Donovan writes:

'This is what I, and others like me, are trying to do 'out there'. Not to bring salvation and goodness and holiness and grace and God, which were there before we got

there. But to bring these people the only thing they did not have before we came – hope – a hope imbedded in the meaning of the life and death and resurrection of Christ. It is a cleansing and humbling thought to see your whole life and work reduced to being simply a channel of hope, and yourself merely a herald of hope, for those who do not have it.' [9]

This requires us to forge relationships with others and to take time to listen to them, without assuming we know best and pushing our agenda and models of faith on them. We also listen *with* them to detect where God is already at work in their life. Being able and willing to listen to, and with, others is a core skill for anyone representing the kingdom of God. If we do it without coming to premature conclusions, we can learn from, and understand our neighbours better. For an ambassador who is a guest and visitor in a foreign land it is a sign of respect and courtesy to listen well and carefully. It is a way of honouring and respecting difference which is central to representing the kingdom.

This kind of honour has its roots in the way of love. It is about valuing others as children of God whether they would identify themselves as that or not. When we speak about a *culture of honour* we must first clarify what we mean. The term has often been associated with what some have termed 'honour killings.' These are carried out largely on young women, by family members who feel they are required to uphold and protect the values that they perceive the woman is violating in some way, perhaps by failing to conform to cultural expectations. It is reasoned that the shame that is brought upon the family by the young woman's violation must be addressed and sometimes this means murder. Elaine Storkey writes:

'International law recognizes honour killing for what it is: a barbaric, brutal and entirely unjustified form of violence, mostly against women, which ruins lives and destroys relationships. It acts as a terrifying deterrent to women who dare to exercise choice over crucial areas of their own lives and futures.' [10]

This is not what I mean when I speak about a culture of honour. To look more closely at our attitudes towards honour we must look at how Jesus talked about it in the Bible.

When Jesus notices how the guests at a dinner party picked the places of honour at the table, He tells them a parable about being invited to a wedding banquet.[11] He says that they should not take the place of honour, because they do not know whether a more distinguished person has been invited. If they choose the best seat they are in danger of being humiliated in public by being asked by their host to move down the table, making room for a more important guest. Instead, they should take the lowest place so that the host may invite them to move up to a better place, and therefore they are honoured in the presence of all the other guests. He finishes the parable by saying:

'For all those who exalt themselves will be humbled, and those who humble themselves will be exalted.' [12]

Looking for honour seems to be a subject that pre-occupies many in the gospels. In Matthew 18 the disciples ask Jesus who is the greatest in the kingdom of heaven. In answer to them, Jesus calls a little child to Him and places the child among them. This is their chance to learn more about kingdom values. He warns them to change and become like little children if they want to enter the kingdom, saying whoever takes the lowly position like a child is the greatest in the kingdom of heaven. [13]

This obviously doesn't give the required learning because the subject doesn't go away. We see in Mark's gospel James and John coming to Jesus seeking places of honour for themselves when Jesus reigns in His kingdom [14] and, in a similar story in Matthew, it's their mother who comes to intercede on their behalf. [15] Jesus makes it clear that it's not His place to choose these positions and He quells the conflict stirred up among the disciples by stating that whoever wants to be great among them must be a servant. [16]

Danny Silk summarises the problem that seeking honour for ourselves has. He writes:

'When honor is expected or even demanded, it becomes just another word for handing the control,

power, and value over to one person in the relationship. A relationship where one person has all the power is one of dishonour, not honour.' [17]

Instead, he describes honour as 'calling out the best in one another.'[18]

Honour is exemplified by an unlikely candidate in Luke's gospel. Here a sex worker gate-crashes a private dinner party so she can anoint Jesus with oil and show her devotion to Him. Instead of being scandalised that such a woman should behave in an intimate way towards a rabbi in a public setting, Jesus honours her. In front of all the guests He contrasts her love and devotion with the lack of care and hospitality expressed by His host. He then forgives her sins and blesses her with peace.[19] I cannot imagine after this scene that there was much appetite to continue the meal. When we challenge a dominant view of what honour looks like and who deserves it is reversed, enemies are created. The more Jesus acts from the values of the kingdom which run against the cultural grain, the more the opposition against Him grows.

Jesus shows what honour looks like by expressing a love and acceptance for those who were considered the least in their society. He eats with 'sinners' and welcomes them. He shows love and care for the powerless and those who are held in low esteem by others. In this way he honours lepers, tax-collectors, women, children, widows, street beggars, sex workers, foreigners, and Roman officials. He sees behind the labels and the assigned status to the individuals made in the image of God. Through His ministry, He demonstrates that the kingdom is an inclusive society. It seeks the welfare of both the outsider and the insider, and we see that in the cycle of parables in Luke 15 about the lost sheep, the lost coin and the lost sons; no one is irrelevant or worthless and God seeks them out Himself. Everyone matters, and Jesus consistently demonstrates His commitment to *the one*. Heidi Baker writes:

'I believe that Jesus would have given His life for just one person. Jesus emptied Himself, He humbled Himself and He so yielded Himself to His Father's love that He had no ambition of His own. He was not looking to build an empire, He did not want praise or adulation or to impress people with who or how many followed Him. He stopped over and over again for just one person, for just one life.' [20]

This is a far cry for the emphasis on numbers and, as we would say in the Church of England, 'bums on pews.' Stopping for the one is a value of The Kingdom. It is seeing the person as God's beloved. When we do this, we mirror His heart for that person. We are not trying to control them or make them believe the same things we do; we are honouring them because God honours them. This culture has healing properties because love transforms and makes us whole, whereas shame fragments and destroys. Shawn Bolz describes the effects of being surrounded by this kind of honouring love. He writes:

'Another wonderful thing about being around people who see you with love is that you forget who you were never meant to be. You forget your self-hatred, shame and fear. You live in your true identity more easily.' [21]

As an ambassador for the kingdom, we have a responsibility to discern what values are shaping our lives. Donald Kraybill describes a way of looking at this by using the image of two ladders side by side. One represents the kingdom of God, and the other, the kingdom of this world. There is an inverted relationship between them, so something that is highly valued on one ladder, ranks near the bottom of the other. He writes:

'Kingdom values challenge the taken-for-granted social ruts and sometimes run against the dominant cultural grain...kingdom values, rooted in the deep love and abiding grace of God, seed new ways of thinking and living. Sometimes the new ways compliment prevailing practices; others times, they don't.' [22]

This is why we have the reversals in the gospels that we have talked about. An ambassador must recognise the distinctive nature of the kingdom that he or she represents. If kingdom values tell us that the last shall be first, the meek shall inherit the earth, and anyone who wants to be great must learn to serve, it follows that ambassadors will at times go against the flow of their host nation's culture if it contradicts kingdom values. Where values are not shared, they stick out. They may incite interest, confusion, anger, or derision, but that isn't really the ambassador's problem. As an outpost of the kingdom, we are called to remain faithful to the reigning culture of our king. This may be very uncomfortable and cost us dearly, but the alternative is to lose the distinctive nature of our citizenship. We do not do this in our own strength but we rely on God making our hearts bigger so we may hold the love that God gives us for all His creation. If we speak of love without real substance to back it up we are like a resounding gong or a clanging cymbal.[23] We have allowed our minds to become too big and our hearts to become too small.

Every value an ambassador for the kingdom expresses is important and these are a summary of what we have covered in this chapter. We honour God's image in everyone and affirm that the Spirit is at work in every place and every person. This does not depend on our recognition or understanding, but on submission to the truth of who God is. We are called to listen to, and listen with, other people, knowing that God already loves and accepts them. We express humility about our mistakes, turning away from our own cultural prejudices and assumed superiority. We encourage new indigenous expressions of Christianity in every culture, without inflicting our control and cultural presumptions. Instead, we are willing to learn from others, whoever they are, knowing that at times our poverty of spirit and ignorance needs correction from those who are richer and wiser.

We follow the pattern of Jesus, learning when to challenge the established value systems with kingdom principles. We are to avoid the big and shiny for its own sake, and instead love God and love the one in front of us.

All these values will help our hearts to swell with kingdom life, but we know where their roots lie, because in all these things, the greatest of these will always be love.[24]

14

THE PRACTICE OF PROCLAMATION

'T*he gospel is the proclamation of the person and work of Jesus Christ and how those benefits can be applied to us by faith alone.*'

R. C. Sproul

'*You are called to be truth-tellers. When truth is proclaimed – all lies, distortions and inferior thinking is revealed for what it is. You are changing your own inner grid system and framework when you are proclaiming My truth.*'

The Ambassador

On the 10th September 2022, after the death of Queen Elizabeth II, an Accession Council was convened at St. James's Palace in order to proclaim

Prince Charles as the new sovereign. At 11 o'clock the Garter King of Arms stood on the balcony of St. James's Palace and read the document to the public proclaiming Charles as monarch. He was surrounded by other Officers of Arms, called Heralds, and the State Trumpeters who sounded the fanfare. It showed us that an official proclamation was required to communicate what had been done and the change that was now upon us all as we welcomed King Charles III's reign.

In the past, proclamation by heralds has been a common way of getting the monarch's message out. One pundit remarked on the televised version that this was 'royal communication circa 1400.' The Accession council had met, the papers had been signed by all the required signatories and now the heralds were there to publish and proclaim what had taken place. It was a typical example of the rich pageantry associated with British history and tradition, it is also helpful as an image of what we're going to be thinking about in this chapter, which is the practice of proclaiming what our king has done.

This is something that Jesus demonstrated in the inauguration of His Ministry in Luke 4:16-31. It was customary for worship leaders in the synagogue to invite a worthy person in the congregation to read from the scriptures and comment on the passage.[1] Jesus unrolls the scroll of Isaiah and reads from Isaiah 61. Jesus reads part of the text that relates to the coming Messiah. There are some fragments of papyrus from the Dead Sea Scrolls at Qumran that explicitly link this passage with the expectation of God's anointed one. These are pre-Christian documents outlining that the Messiah will preach good news to the poor, provide release for the captives, open the eyes of the blind and raise up the downtrodden. Another fragment says that the Holy Spirit rests on the Messiah.[2]

If we compare the contents of Isaiah 61 and the story of Jesus reading it at Nazareth told in Luke 4, we can see that there are some differences. This isn't about the translator getting it wrong or the story changing over time, this is a deliberate act. The *Mishnah* is the earliest collection of the sayings of the Jewish rabbis, dating from about 100 B.C.E to 200 C.E when it was compiled. In it are rabbinic rules about how to read scripture in the synagogue, and the reading of Isaiah 61 recorded in Luke 4 falls within these guidelines.

The reader is required to recite the Torah as it is written, but if the passage is from the Prophets, one is allowed to leave out verses. How much is omitted will depend on the flow. The stipulations require that the interpreter should be left with no time to make a pause in the translation. We may wonder where the idea of an interpreter comes from, but as the scrolls are in Hebrew and most of those in the synagogue only understood Aramaic, an interpreter must stand beside the reader and translate. This practice of editing allows for a reader to turn to a verse somewhere else in the book and insert it seamlessly in the flow after the translator speaks. Then the reader returns to the original passage.[3]

What Jesus does in Luke 4 is to omit one phrase, borrow a second from Isaiah 58:6 and cut the final sentence in half. His editing focuses on proclamation, justice, advocacy, and compassion. When He speaks of proclaiming 'the year of the Lord's favour', He is using the language of *Jubilee*. In the Sabbatical year (every seventh year) the land is left fallow, slaves are released, and debts are cancelled. Then after seven Sabbatical years, there is a year of Jubilee. This fiftieth year is dedicated to rest, once again to releasing people from debts, servitude and slavery, and the land is to be returned to its original owners at the start of the fifty-year period to prevent greedy landlords taking advantage of their poor tenant farmers.[4]

Although it is difficult to know how carefully these practices were observed over Israel's history, Jesus is using language that people understood. Jubilee is a response to God's gracious liberation and deliverance.[5] It is passing on God's goodness. Then, in a way of proclaiming who He is and what His ministry is all about, He rolls up the scroll, gives it back, sits down and says:

'Today this scripture is fulfilled in your hearing.' [6]

Although the translation we usually read in response to this bombshell is *'all spoke well of him,'* some scholars suggest that the key words in the Greek text can be translated more negatively. The way that the story unfolds suggests that the crowd are against Him and are envious and demeaning of 'Joseph's son' who cannot be taken seriously.[7] The argument that the crowd are against Jesus straight away is supported by the fact that, in His reading, He stops at the point when judgement is pronounced on the Gentiles. The crowd have been waiting for this punchline and then the expected vengeance is removed. Kenneth Bailey paraphrases what he thinks verse 22, which starts with *'all spoke well of him,'* really means:

'What is the matter with this boy? He has quoted one of our favourite texts but has omitted some of its most important verses. In the process he has turned a text of judgment into a text of mercy. This is outrageous! The Messianic age is a golden age for us and a day of God's vengeance upon them. How could this boy grow up here and not know this? Doesn't he remember why this village was founded?' [8]

The hostility grows even stronger when Jesus then gives examples of Gentiles which God chose to bless *instead* of Israel.[9] This would have stirred up strong nationalist feelings and it's not surprising that some are furious at this 'blasphemer' and want to throw Him off the cliff. Bailey writes:

'When a land-grabbing venture is in progress, woe to the brave soul who dares select models of faith from among the victims, especially when the aggressors are certain that God is on their side. From this day forward Jesus knows that his message and person will continue to trigger deep and violent hostility.' [10]

Jesus demonstrates the inclusive nature of the kingdom, referring to the faith and value of Gentiles in a Jewish synagogue, and honouring examples of both a man and a woman within a male dominated context. This is not just about fulfilling nationalist hopes, this is a new era with a universal message of grace. The Jubilee restoration isn't just for Jews, it's for everyone and it's happening now in front of their eyes.

This passage has been called *The Nazareth Manifesto* because it highlights the shape of mission and ministry of Jesus, both then and now. Sam Wells explains how the challenge and comfort of Jesus comes to each person. He writes:

'Jesus' presence fulfils all the promises of Isaiah. It is a call to each person and to the occupied land of Israel – to recognise that they are poor, that they are in prison, that their body is in prison, that they are oppressed, that they cannot hide their lies and deceit from God. It is an invitation to each person, and to the nation, to be set free, to open their life to the most powerful force in the world, to receive forgiveness from God and one another, to enter the Jubilee year – today. It is a procla-

mation of the hope that lies in the words, "God is with us." [11]

The passage in Luke 4 helps us to see how Jesus understood His mission at the time. He was fulfilling the role of the Jewish Messiah but not necessarily in the way that it was understood by some of the home crowd. The purposes of God far outstripped any parochial sense of favouritism and exclusivity, and we see this repeatedly in Jesus' ministry. He is not afraid to challenge societal prejudices by crossing the lines and recognised boundaries with the love and grace of God. While He never deserts His Jewish identity and heritage, He says:

'I have other sheep that are not of this sheepfold. I must bring them also. They too will listen to my voice, and there shall be one flock and one shepherd.' [12]

This is foreshadowing the move of the Gospel to encompass the Gentiles and grafting them into the vine,[13] which is a symbol of the House of Israel. This story develops throughout the New Testament with the early disciples, and then missionaries throughout the centuries who have spread the good news of Jesus to the nations of the world. The Nazareth Manifesto continues to shape and form our understanding today.

When I was training for ministry, I spent some time in the chaplaincy of a Christian-based hospital that not only provided excellent medical care, but concentrated on well-being in terms of mind, body, and spirit. We offered services of healing with a simple liturgy and prayers. I remember the Chaplain saying to me that when I was praying for people at the altar rail that it would be good to focus on what Jesus' mission was, and still is, and he pointed to the Luke 4:18-19 passage as a guide. It reinforced the fact that God does not change. He is still interested in proclaiming good news to the poor, freedom for the prisoners, recovery of sight for the blind, setting the oppressed free, and declaring the time of the Lord's favour.

We also have the benefit of looking back, not just at the ministry of Jesus, but His death and resurrection and in particular, the last words He says as He dies on the cross:

'Later, knowing that everything had now been finished, and so that Scripture would be fulfilled, Jesus said, 'I am thirsty.' A jar of wine vinegar was there, so they soaked a sponge in it, put the sponge on a stalk of the hyssop plant, and lifted it to Jesus' lips. When he had received the drink, Jesus said, 'It is finished.' With that, he bowed his head and gave up his spirit.' [14]

It is completed. Or as Robert Powell movingly says in the television mini-series, *Jesus of Nazareth,* 'It is accomplished.' *The Passion Translation* of John 19 verse 30 adds *'It is finished, my bride!'* The Hebrew word *kalah* is a word that can mean 'fulfilled or completed' but also 'bride'. There are references in the Bible to Jesus being the Bridegroom, John the

Baptist being the friend or Best Man to the Groom, and the whole Church being the Bride of Christ.[15] The translators have combined both concepts and add a note in the commentary:

'Although the completed work of salvation was finished on the cross, [Jesus] continues to work through his church today to extend God's kingdom realm on the earth and glorify the Father through us. He continues to work in us to accomplish all that His cross and resurrection have purchased for us, his bride. His cross fulfilled and finished the prophecies of the Messiah's first coming to earth. There was nothing written that was not fulfilled and now offered to His bride.' [16]

Whether combining these two concepts enriches our understanding or not, the point made is that something has been fulfilled by Jesus' death. If He fulfilled the prophecy about the Messiah's ministry from Isaiah 61 when He was living, by His death and resurrection He has now fulfilled something on a cosmic scale. Understanding this, as much as we are able, is both the challenge for faith and academic theology. It is also directly related to the role of an ambassador. *The Passion Translation* interprets 2 Corinthians 5: 20 like this:

'We are ambassadors of the Anointed One who carry the message of Christ to the world, as though God were tenderly pleading with them directly through our lips. So we tenderly plead with you on Christ's behalf, "Turn back to God and be reconciled to him." [17]

To ensure that we speak on Christ's behalf, we must recognise what He has achieved through the cross. For this to live within me as a reality, I have to unpack it and assimilate it into my language and understanding. It's important that it feels natural rather than 'stuck on' with words and concepts that are more at home in the academic field than my earthy vernacular.

This took me back to my two-way journaling and a conversation I was having with God. I wanted to know from God whether there was anything else I needed to do to see the answers to a particular prayer. I was also preparing for what the Church calls 'Safeguarding Sunday', which is about focusing on our responsibility to ensure the well-being of those we come into contact with, particularly the most vulnerable. As I was preparing a sermon that could potentially re-trigger trauma in those who have been abused or neglected, I wanted to be very careful and to seek God's take on it. My journal records the flow of the answer:

'I've heard your prayers, Mandy, and already there is action in the heavenly realms. Do not think that your prayer will be heard due to its many words; it is the intention of your heart that matters. I see that and respond to that; now rest in Me. You cannot make something happen; it is My work transforming your thoughts and words into action. Now it's about resting

in what you know about My character, My love for my
children, and My power which is made perfect in your
weakness.

What is it that you know about My heart for My
children on Safeguarding Sunday?

- I keep coming back to the fact that You
  have come to set the prisoners free and
  release the oppressed. There is nothing
  like fear, lies, denial and abuse to keep
  people captive. It's Your heart to liberate
  them.

'That's right. So always remember this was on My
heart first before it was on yours; it was My decree before
it was yours. You are not trying to persuade Me or
change My mind. You are following Me, not the other
way around. What else?'

- That You care for Your children more
  than I do, or ever could. That it is Your
  longing that has been expressed through
  scripture and through Jesus. He is the
  model bringing everything into
  wholeness. He came to undo and destroy
  the works of the evil one and He
  accomplished it. 'It is
  finished/accomplished;' so He's already
  done everything needed to bring

deliverance and healing. It's His work - we just get to be ambassadors of it.

'YES! – Now you see it. You get it. An ambassador is there to represent the power he or she represents/stands for. You stand for Me. It is my power that you have and you release it, not because you work up to it. I've already given you the kingdom. Can you feel the shift? This is a shift in perception. The work has been done. I'm just waiting for those to release it.

I have been waiting for some of My children to realise this. 'It is finished' means just that. You stand in transferred power. I have done it and I give My children the finished work of Christ through the Holy Spirit. Trust Me and invite Me as a channel of grace for all My children.'

While I believe that Jesus has done all the work, some application is still required. We are invited into partnership with Him and therefore one of the things that we are asked to do is to proclaim His works. We have been authorised to speak on His behalf and invested with royal power through the name of Jesus. God reminded me in the journaling that I was living and speaking *from* truth, not *for* it. It is His pleasure to give His children the kingdom[18] and the kingdom comes through mysterious and wonderful, miraculous and supernatural signs and through the small, everyday things of life. Not everything arrives with a fanfare but that doesn't mean that it's not an authentic sign of the kingdom breaking in. Sometimes we just don't have the eyes to see it.

When we take seriously the role of an ambassador to speak on behalf of the Sovereign, our speech becomes less timid. We have kingdom authority to speak and command for Him.[19] Jane Hamon encourages us to practice speaking out declarations and decrees that align with God's heart. She says:

'When we agree with the voice of God and verbalize what He is saying, we are given the power to shift heaven and earth and change our very circumstances with prophetic declarations. These authoritative, spiritually empowered decrees have the capacity to bring breakthrough and initiate change.' [20]

This may seem a bold claim about a practice that many Christians might not feel comfortable with, but it rests on the power of God's words. We know that God speaks Creation into being in the story in Genesis, and we also see the authoritative manner Jesus uses when He brings healing to people. He doesn't make lengthy prayers to His father for healing; He commands it. We see it in 'Stretch out your hand; be made whole; take up your bed and walk; Lazarus come out!'. These are strong words not asking permission or suggesting.

We may think 'well that's okay for Jesus but we're not Him.' That is true, but an ambassador functions as their country's representative. They speak on behalf of their homeland, putting into words the views and policies of their government or monarch. We see this in the world of global politics when ambassadors are called to account for their country's actions. Most recently we have seen many diplomats being expelled from Russian Embassies around the world in retaliation for the war in Ukraine. Embassy staff are seen as an extension of the country that they represent. The host nation therefore gives a clear message to the ambassador's homeland about their policies by responding to embassy staff *as if* they were the country itself. This shows the power that an ambassador holds, even if this only comes through association with their home nation. In less troubled times an ambassador can wield enormous influence because of this representative role.

This influence is ours too when God invites us to act for Him and speak His words to transform lives. Jane Hamon writes:

'We are God's ambassadors in this world, and what we speak and declare causes His kingdom to come and His will to be done, on earth as it is in heaven.' [21]

One of the things that God was teaching me during this period was the need to listen for His voice. The two-way journaling provided an immediate method of intentionally making time to do this, but it was also about listening to Him through His words in the Bible. Both could be fashioned into declarations, proclaiming what the Lord has done. Jane Hamon explains her practice:

'We must marry the power of prayer and the authority of the decree. Prayer is our petitions, communication and fellowship with God, while decrees are God's words released through our voices into the earth realm to bring change. These words, which can be scripture or prophetic words or promises we receive from the Lord are formed into declarations and spoken out loud.' [22]

Jane Hamon and others who promote the use of declarations and decrees argue that the power of speaking out God's words not only encourages faith, in speaker and listeners, but it changes the atmosphere. In Isaiah it says that God's words cannot return to Him without accomplishing what He desires and achieving the purpose for which He sent them.[23] When we are speaking out God's words, we are hearing the truth of His heart and there is transforming power contained in the process.

I asked Abba to teach me about proclamation, how the practice of declaring and speaking decrees out loud was part of the role of an ambassador, and how this may lead to the kingdom breaking through. This is the response I received.

'Let Me show you first in My Word. Jesus proclaimed that Isaiah 61 was fulfilled in their hearing. He was doing it, and He was already showing that blind eyes were seeing, the deaf ears were hearing, and the lame were

walking. He was proclaiming what He was doing. This is a testimony.

You are in Him and He is in you, so you already have within you all that you need in Jesus to do the things He has done. You have read about it in Heidi and Rolland's book, you have read about the word of testimony that Bill Johnson has written about. These people are moving in my signs and wonders because they know what I have done, I can do again, over, and over, and I can do more than you imagine.

Too big a mind and too little a heart gets in the way. You stop and rationalise away a miracle before it begins to take hold. You also expect it to fall into your lap fully formed when sometimes it arrives in seed form. Giving you miracles does not necessarily grow your relationship with Me. It makes you a thrill-seeker, someone who runs off with the present without spending time with the Giver. That will only bring about an immature, demanding dynamic like a child who gets his/her own way too easily. I am committed to your character. I long to give you good things and to delight you, and My grace is all there for you waiting. I will not deny you, but I am just as committed to your growth and maturity so you can steward what I give you well.

I do not want to give you something that will over-whelm you to the point of warping my message. What I say to you is position your heart to receive My wisdom about declaration and the coming Glory. Position your heart to be ready, knowing that everything is already in your account because of Jesus. Focus on what My Son has done and therefore what He has already given you in the inheritance of His completed work. Lean into this. Hold fast to this. Make space to receive.

- I understand this Lord, but what does it mean in practical steps? How do I 'go lower' as the Bakers would say? How do I position my heart and be ready? I feel you've been talking about resting when I feel positioning my heart means something active. Will You explain it to me? What does it mean to have this hunger and desire but also to rest in You? It feels like a contradiction.

'I want you to focus on the work of the cross. I keep bringing you back to the words 'It is finished' – this is true - but I call you into partnership to proclaim this. This is part of the process. You are not labouring for Me, you are declaring what has been done, and all its benefits are available – that is the proclamation. Changing hearts and minds comes into being by a relationship with My truth.

You are called to be truth-tellers. When truth is proclaimed – all lies, distortions and inferior thinking is revealed for what it is. You are changing your own inner grid system and framework when you are proclaiming My truth. Lean into this and let My truth lighten any darkness and shape all that you think and believe. Faith grows, Love blossoms, Hope arises. You do not strive, you receive the truth in rest – but it gives you what is needed, My truth in your mind and heart creating kingdom life that will glow from you as you live inside out.'

I resolved that I would practice proclaiming what God has done, not just for me but for everyone. It is the natural work of an Evangelist but with it comes the power of prophecy, for what God has done, He can do again, and who doesn't want to hear that God can still save, heal, and deliver us all?

15

RE-WIRING REQUIRED

'*O*ur brain is changing moment by moment as we are thinking. By our thinking and choosing, we are redesigning the landscape of our brain.'

Dr. Caroline Leaf

'It is important to remember that opinion is not the same as truth. This can be difficult to hear when loud and influential voices around us are not making the distinction.'

The Ambassador

In this chapter we're going to be exploring further how our words create our worlds and how we begin to bring our thinking into alignment with

God's. It makes sense that if we are to represent God then it presupposes that we will be in constant communication with Him and know what His mind is on things. We then hit the obstacle that most of us do not think like God. It highlights that one of the greatest battlegrounds is the mind. Shawn Bolz sums up God's desire in these words:

'He wants to reveal his nature to you and rewire your brain with kingdom thinking and living. He wants to make your heart full and whole and help you to make the best decisions you can, not make them for you. That is why Jesus spoke in parables; he was changing the perspective of everyone around him to see from heaven's culture rather than earth's. He wanted to realign their heart attitudes and relational skillsets with those of heaven.' [1]

Unfortunately, when we talk about *re-wiring*, some people naturally become suspicious as if we are talking about some cult 'brainwashing' its adherents. I came across this when talking with a family who were asking for their child to be christened. We have a very open baptism policy at the church with few hurdles that the family are expected to leap over. We do, however, want them to know what baptism is about and for the promises made to have some integrity behind them. We want to encourage every movement towards faith, however small, even when the words of the baptism service don't match up with the extent of the family's engagement with the

Christian faith. In my experience, most don't want to be offered a Thanksgiving Service for their child instead of baptism. They want the 'real deal' with the water and the font. Many also interpret the requirement to attend baptism classes as putting obstacles in their way and a sign of the church being unwelcoming to them. Although I never know whether we get it right, I always err on the side of grace. I know that God can turn anything around.

In the Church of England, when a child is too young to speak for themselves, their parents and appointed Godparents speak on their behalf. They promise that they will encourage the child's Christian faith by example, so that they can find their place within the life and worship of the Church.[2] I remember asking a family whether they were willing to support this. The mother told me that she didn't want to 'indoctrinate' the child but for them to make up their mind when they were older. While I support the importance of choice, I wonder how a child can decide about the Christian faith and the Church without knowledge and experience. How do they know what they are accepting or rejecting if they never show up? It was as if the family believed that an experience of faith would be imparted solely by osmosis in the font! Nevertheless, we welcomed them, hoping that God's grace would encourage a foundation for later faith development. The experience taught me that this fear of indoctrination reveals a level of brainwashing already at work from another source.

Indoctrination is usually associated with religion or political ideology, but it's much wider and more pervasive than that. According to the Cambridge dictionary the word means:

'the process of repeating an idea or belief to someone until they accept it without criticism or question.'[3]

What we don't always recognise is the many subtle ways we are indoctrinated, and how in some areas of our lives it's already happened. It may come through advertising, the media, through our peer group and education. So often our indoctrination is hiding in plain sight but because we do not perceive it for what it is, it just becomes part of us and it is accepted without question. Much of what we think about ourselves is just that. The family culture in which we grew up is probably the most significant influence we have had, but also our schooling and our friendship groups play a major part. All contribute to what we have learned about our identity and value, and all affect our levels of confidence and well-being. It is important to remember that opinion is not the same as truth. This can be difficult to hear when loud and influential voices around us are not making the distinction.

Developing critical faculties to challenge and question what we've been taught is one of the tasks of adolescence and adulthood. We also need space, time, and possibly on occasion, more skilled help to discern what belongs to us and what doesn't. With enough corrective experiences we can leave behind the old skin that we've grown out of and feel freer and more comfortable with who God made us to be.

The word 'indoctrination' holds negative connotations but there are positive aspects to modelling behaviour for others. No one would complain if a child learned to be kind or generous because they witnessed a parent being so, and there are lots of habits and preferences that can be passed on by social learning. My father is a life-long Charlton Athletic supporter and when our first son was born his grandfather bought him a bib with the words 'I dribble for Charlton' printed on it. After regular trips to the Valley to watch the game and enough re-enforcement given, both of our sons are now ardent Charlton Athletic fans.

All of us are influenced by what we read, watch, or take part in. We may think we are starting from a 'neutral' position (whatever that means) but the truth is we will have already observed responses from others and absorbed their opinions. The more important someone is to us in our social network, the more we are likely to listen to their opinion and give it credence. We learn from those around us, and others in turn, learn from us. Even when we think there is freedom to choose, there are always power dynamics and social influences at play suggesting that none of us are as independently minded as we think we are.

Contrary to the suspicion that engaging with faith is a form of brainwashing, it may be argued that our critical faculties are, in fact, sharpened by it. The learning that is part of our engagement with scripture, the reading of different commentaries and authors, and the Spirit of Truth within us that oversees our understanding, causes us to think. We are encouraged to question and weigh up different views, rather than just swallow down chunks of scripture without thought. In the Jewish tradition and the practice of the rabbis, questions form an integral part where heart and mind work together. We can see this in the way Jesus often answers a question by posing another question because there is much to unravel. However, it's the heart's response that carries the greater weight in the end.

In this engagement there is always choice. Without choice there is only control, and control violates the freedom that is required in love. Therefore, even in the Genesis account we read that there are lots of fruit trees in the garden that Adam and Eve can eat from. The only one they must not eat the fruit of is the tree of the knowledge of good and evil.[4] This is giving them a choice to obey God or go their own way. Without that choice they are not fully loved. We read of the choice again in Deuteronomy:

'I have set before you life and death, blessings and

curses. *Now choose life, so that you and your children may live..'* [5]

Dr. Caroline Leaf is a cognitive neuroscientist and, in her book, *Switch On Your Brain,* [6] she explains how our ability to think and choose sculpts the landscape of our brain. We build branches and networks through the firing and wiring together of neurons. This brain activity can be monitored in a number of ways. She states:

'Just the mind activity from your reading of the next few lines generates electromagnetic, electrochemical, and quantum action in your neurons. It causes magnetic fields that can be measured; electrical impulses that can be tracked; chemical effects that can be seen and measured; photons to be activated that can be captured on computer screens; energy activity that can be explained using quantum physics; and vibrations in the membranes of the neurons that can be picked up by instrumentation.' [7]

What Dr. Leaf argues is that even those things that we might presume are just part of us and unchangeable, such as our genes, can be modified by our choices. The mind shapes the brain, and this neuroplasticity may work for us, or against us, depending on what we think about the most. Connections may be built and strengthened or weakened and fall into disuse.

A good analogy is to think about a bypass being built. In one of my previous parishes, there was one main road through the village. This meant there was a high volume of traffic going through it with its associated exhaust fumes and safety issues. The road was damaged through extensive use and journey times had to be amended because of the traffic jams that occurred. However, when a bypass was built, it diverted the through traffic away from the village road to the dual carriageway. It freed up the village to become a more pleasant place to live and the drivers benefitted from the faster, wider, and less congested road. Building new neural connections is like creating different routes in our brain that affect the expression of our genes, our behaviour, and our well-being.

The Apostle Paul writes to the church in Rome saying:

'Do not conform to the pattern of this world but be transformed by the renewing of your mind. Then you will be able to test and approve what God's will is – his good, pleasing and perfect will.' [8]

When Paul talks about renewing the mind, his advice does not sound like indoctrination. Instead, it points to the need for critical analysis. First, we are to discern what the pattern of 'this world' is. Secondly, there is the process of recognising the difference following Jesus makes to this pattern. Then finally, further testing is required so that the Roman Christians can discern God's will. It is a given that when Paul talks about transformation, it involves the work of God's Spirit not human effort alone.

Christians are called to engage the process of renewing our minds if we are to represent the kingdom in the place that He has put us. If we go with the flow of surrounding cultures then there will be occasions when we are working against the character and nature of the kingdom. We might not realise that every time, but there will be occasions when we feel some discomfort about our choices, or confusion about what to do.

Re-wiring begins with recognising that we need to do some work. Like a house in need of renovation, a survey reveals what is not fit for purpose. Although it is a big job, if there's faulty wiring it is dangerous and it needs to be renewed. Our neural networks are not so different from that house. We are all in need of renovation. Paul's advice to the Roman Christians could help us here as we reflect on the patterns in cultures around us, the difference our discipleship with Jesus makes, and further testing and approving of God's will. All of this is in partnership with the Holy Spirit, who leads us into all truth.[9]

This process of renewal can be uncomfortable because it will at times require us to go against our cultural conditioning. It will reveal unconscious, as well as conscious, biases. Keeping our head down and not rocking the boat may seem attractive to avoid drawing attention to ourselves and escape conflict, but this is not what being a disciple means. I remember seeing a T-Shirt with the words "Only dead fish go with the flow" printed on it. It seems apt for this chapter.

When we look at the three years of Jesus' ministry recorded in the Gospels, we can see a catalogue of conflicts and challenges as the kingdom of light clashes with the domain of darkness and sinful human nature. Jesus is not afraid to be direct with people and stir things up. The Apostle Peter picks up the earlier reference in Isaiah when he writes in his first letter that Jesus is:

'A stone that causes people to stumble and a rock that makes them fall.' [10]

Jesus makes a habit of revealing truth and that is challenging for everyone. When things that are hidden come to the surface, only those who want to be cleansed from their wrongdoing and set free welcome it. Those who don't want to be exposed, or who cannot see their own faults, will turn on the one who is revealing them. Being a truth-teller in these circumstances does not lead to keeping under the radar and living a quiet life. Instead, everywhere Jesus goes He rocks the boat. He challenges the status quo and this inevitably confronts existing power structures and those with privilege. His words and actions are an offence to many, and He becomes the stumbling block to their entry into the kingdom. This opposition grows until it reaches its height with

Jesus' crucifixion. God's truth comes at a cost and Jesus is very clear about taking up our cross when we follow Him. [11]

Not all people with power and privilege in the Gospels have closed minds and hearts, however. Some respond with insight and humility. We have Nicodemus the Pharisee[12] who comes to Jesus at night to discuss what it means to be born again. We have the Roman Centurion who believes that, like him, Jesus is a man of authority and only has to say the word and his servant will be healed.[13] There is Joseph of Arimathea, a rich man who became a disciple and then gives his tomb to Jesus[14] (which must have been the shortest occupancy in history). Then, scratching under the surface a little, there is Joanna, who is named as one of the women who goes to the tomb to anoint Jesus' body.[15] We learn elsewhere in Luke's gospel that she is the wife of Chuza, the manager of King Herod's household. She supports Jesus and the disciples financially out of her own means.[16] Here we have people with power and influence responding positively to the message of Jesus. It is not just the poor and the powerless who become disciples. It may be easier for those who have less to see the treasure of the Gospel, but other hearts are open too.

Whether we have power and influence in this world or not, being followers of Jesus means that we walk in His footsteps, and this can draw us into becoming a counter-cultural community. We are a new band that marches to the beat of a different drum. As Donald Kraybill writes:

'Citizens of the new kingdom have a different vision, a different set of values. They pledge allegiance to a different king. And at times that allegiance means they will sail against the prevailing social winds.' [17]

With every shift into becoming an outpost of what Kraybill calls, *The Upside-Down Kingdom,* we put ourselves in the firing line. This is not a comfortable place to be but it is part of the prophetic call upon the Church to speak truth to power. It requires confidence in the message of the Gospel. We need followers of Jesus to be the Josephs of Arimatheas and the Joannas to work in places of influence in our world, but we are also called to speak for *and with* the forgotten, the invisible, the powerless, and the outcasts. Heidi Baker writes:

'As we look with His heart and His eyes to the lost, the broken, the empty, the orphans, those who have had everything they have taken from them, as we start to put them first, doing nothing to promote ourselves, but doing everything out of His love and for His glory – then we are becoming more like Him, Jesus, who gave up everything to become like us.' [18]

When I read this quotation from Heidi Baker, I am deeply challenged. I can see how far I fall from this goal. This is why renewing the mind begins with repentance. It requires us to turn away from what may seem natural to us from our inculturation in the world and turn towards the mind of Christ.[19] What the Apostle Paul says to the Corinthians is that those who have the Spirit possess the Messiah's mind. We are therefore open to the truth that is not reliant on mere human wisdom.[20] We are encouraged to work with the Holy Spirit in the task of re-wiring our minds.

Dr. Caroline Leaf describes what the process of change looks like from a cognitive neuroscience viewpoint. She states that this is based on regular exercising of our brain and this takes place over time through continual persistence.[21] She writes about a cycle of twenty-one days for all the protein changes to happen to create a long-term integrated memory. However, if we stop thinking about something after four or five days, which is common, then the memory dies and becomes heat energy. In short, we forget it.[22] Renewing our mind, therefore, is a process of rewiring the nerve networks in our brain, getting rid of toxic thinking, and replacing it with healthy thoughts. She states:

'To detox your thought life, you need to remember it's your thinking that will actually change your brain. So you need to do consciously what your mind does on a nonconscious level to build a thought. You control your brain; your brain does not control you.' [23]...*'Wherever there is more thinking activity, there will be more wiring.'*[24]

This practice is exemplified in Philippians 4 when Paul writes:

'Finally, brothers and sisters, whatever is true, whatever is noble, whatever is right, whatever is pure, whatever is lovely, whatever is admirable – if anything is excellent or praiseworthy – think about such things.' [25]

Richard Rohr also writes about the part our focus plays in renewing our mind or entertaining toxic thoughts. He states that neuroscience tells us that fear, negativity, and hatred stick like Velcro to the nerves, while positivity, gratitude and appreciation slide away like Teflon from those same nerves – until we savour them or choose them for a minimum of a conscious fifteen seconds, only then do they imprint[26]. He reminds his readers that:

'The positive, loving and non-argumentative savoring of the moment is called contemplation.' [27]

Although cognitive neuroscience may be a modern discipline, those who meditated on the truth of scripture and practiced contemplation were clearly modelling the way to renew their minds before science could explain it.

The mind is a constant battleground for those who want to follow Jesus because we live *in* the world but are not *of* it. We have been socially conditioned by our surrounding cultures whether we realise it or not, and at times this is at odds with kingdom values. Even when we think we are living kingdom culture, it is more an amalgamation of

different models that we have not sufficiently ques-
tioned. It is only when we recognise how different
the culture of the kingdom is from what we perceive
as 'normal' around us, do we realise how much
distance we have yet to travel. Thank goodness for
the grace of God!

Kraybill writes about the habits of the kingdom
community, stating:

*'Love replaces hate among us. Shalom overcomes
revenge. We love even enemies. Basins replace swords in
our society. We share power, love assertively, and make
peace. We flatten hierarchies and behave like children.
Compassion replaces personal ambition among us.
Equality overshadows competition and achievement.
Obedience to Jesus blots out worldly charm. Servant
structures replace rigid bureaucracies...Generosity,
Jubilee, mercy, and compassion – these are the marks of
the new community. Freed from the grip of right-side-up
kingdoms, we salute a new King and sing a new song. We
transcend earthly borders, boundaries, and passports. We
pledge allegiance to a new and already-present
kingdom.'*[28]

In partnership with the Holy Spirit, we are
invited to re-wire our circuits in a thorough conversion. It's a journey of a lifetime that involves our
minds and hearts, bodies and spirits. It is part of our
transformation where we become more like the One
we follow, and are changed 'from one degree of glory
to another'.[29]

16

THE SEAL OF THE LAMB

'Good works are the seals and proofs of faith; for even as a letter must have a seal to strengthen the same, even so faith must have good works.'

Martin Luther

'This time I was carrying release papers for the prisoners with The Seal of The Lamb on them, validating them and giving me the authority to act as an ambassador to the King.'

The Ambassador

After nearly six weeks of freedom, another migraine struck. I felt it coming on and I tried to shake it off by drinking lots of water, spraying topical magnesium on my neck and shoulders and purpose-fully relaxing but it established itself properly in the night and I had a fitful sleep. However, as it seems to happen, I had a very powerful dream that woke me up properly.

I had been working on this book and thinking about a cover for it. I was looking at stock images of red wax seals on scrolls and parchment. I was thinking how ambassadors in previous centuries would have received letters from their homeland with a wax seal securing and authenticating it. Some officials would have their own seal, sometimes as a separate stamp, or used the impression of the family crest or symbol from a signet ring to confirm who the sender was. Seals of different kinds are still used today, particularly when the document is a legal one.

I was reminded in the dream of the service we had when I took office as the vicar of my parish. There are legal requirements under church law, (known as canon law) in a service of Institution. One of these is for a licence to be given by the bishop to the minister to preach and carry out ecclesiastical duties. This is called *licensing of ministers under seal*.[1] A document is prepared with the bishop's seal and signature on it admitting the minister into the parish. The canon requires that during the service:

'The bishop, when [he] gives institution, shall read the words of institution from a written instrument having the episcopal seal appended thereto; and during

the reading thereof the priest who is to be instituted shall kneel before the bishop and hold the seal in [his] hand.' [2]

When the licence is given to the minister the bishop says:

'Receive this cure of souls which is both yours and mine.'

The Bishop of Oxford, Steven Croft, states:

'The cure of souls we are given is, of course, of the whole parish and benefice. The term cure means more than care (although all cure of souls is built on love). At its centre is the ministry of reconciliation between individuals and God and between people and communities through the death and resurrection of Jesus Christ.' [3]

What this means is that we are sharing the care of all those in our parish with the bishop. We have his or her authority to do so and the licence is authenticated by their seal and signature. The reason why I was brought back to this experience of being made vicar is that in my dream I saw the Seal of Jesus on a document. It was an impression in red wax of the *Agnus Dei* - the 'Lamb of God'.

In the Hebrew Scriptures there is particular emphasis on lambs being offered in sacrifice to take away sin. Only lambs 'without blemish' were to be chosen for this offering.[4] Although the whole concept of animal sacrifice for human wrongdoing seems hideous to our modern ears, to ancient cultures this was a way of life. John the Baptist first describes Jesus as the Lamb of God who takes away sins of the world when he sees Him among the crowds coming for baptism.[5] The image looks back to the scripture in Isaiah 53: 7-8 where God's unnamed Suffering Servant is described as a lamb silent before its slaughter. This picture is again picked up by the Apostle Peter in his first letter when he states:

'For you know that it was not with perishable things such as silver or gold that you were redeemed from the empty way of life handed down to you from your ancestors, but with the precious blood of Christ, a lamb without blemish or defect.' [6]

There are also a number of references to the lamb in the book of Revelation.[7] In chapter 5 we read how thousands upon thousands are worshipping the lamb 'who was slain,' and is worthy to receive power and wealth and wisdom and strength and honour and glory and praise'[8]

The Lamb of God has been a popular subject on which to compose many pieces of beautiful sacred music. In a previous parish, I would sing as part of our Communion liturgy, *'Lamb of God, who takes away the sin of the world, have mercy on us.'*

Early Christian art, sculpture, and mosaic commonly contained images of a lamb to represent Jesus. Then after a church council in 692 C.E. there was a shift away from animals representing Christ[9] as the Council wanted artists to engage with the reality of Jesus as a human being. However, the

Agnus Dei still persisted with Francisco de Zurbarán's oil on canvas *'The Bound Lamb'*[10] being one of the most famous.

In my dream I saw The Seal of The Lamb. It was in the style of a lamb standing up with its foreleg around a long stemmed cross with a banner hanging from it, with a St. George's style cross on the flag. After seeing the seal, I found myself re-entering the dream I had in the Epilogue of *The Beach* and the one I wrote about in the introduction of this book. This time I was carrying release papers for the prisoners with The Seal of The Lamb on them, validating them and giving me the authority to act as an ambassador to the king.

I was awake by now and kept repeating "I have seen The Seal, I have seen The Seal." I knew there was unfinished business here, so I followed the pattern of the previous dream that had been etched on my mind. I put in my ear plugs to listen to the sounds of the beach to remind me that the Holy Trinity was with me and would never leave me, and with my official papers I went down into the dark place.

I arrived at the inside of an extremely tall, grey tower. It was as high as a skyscraper. Filling the space was a giant who was roaring and moving around in a confined space. I saw his feet and thought that one of his toes could easily crush me. He didn't take any notice of me though. This reminded me of a phrase I had read in a book by Jane Hamon about *Declarations for Breakthrough.* She states:

'I believe this season will be characterized by gates, Goliaths and glory. Go through the gates, defeat your Goliaths and then step into His glory.' [11]

In the entrance to the tower there was a desk, and a man came to speak to me. He looked familiar, like an actor I'd seen, and I showed him the seal I had on the papers. He eyed me suspiciously and asked whether it was genuine and tried to persuade me I had got it wrong. I knew he was lying, so I took no notice of him and went through the other door opposite the entrance. I was following directions from the Trinity of where I needed to go. I saw someone I knew in the cells who called out to me but I knew I had to keep going and would come back again to see her.

I kept going until I saw a little girl who looked about three years old in a cell with a man who she was clearly afraid of. The man was alternately crying out for help and then manifesting as a demon who was keeping him captive. When he was a man, he presented as weak and pathetic but he couldn't get free. The little girl looked scared and sad, and she had something hanging on her which was heavy. I wondered who was tormenting who more by their presence. I held the little girl's hand through the bars and asked her if she wanted to go. She said she did. I told her that she needed to forgive the man first to escape him. I explained this wasn't about 'letting him off'; this was about releasing him to Jesus, refusing to punish, and cutting herself off from him. So, with help from me, she said *"I release you from your offence, I forgive you and leave you to the Lord."* The cell was already unlocked and she came out and into my arms where I held her. The man stayed in his cell, a pathetic creature captive to the demon who controlled him. The entity that had hung around the little girl could not stay; it fell to the ground and crept away.

Awake and yet still suffering from the migraine, I drew a picture of the seal in my two-way journal and created a WhatsApp group for morning prayer telling them that I was unwell and I wouldn't be there.

Hilary, one of our number, wrote a few minutes later that she wanted to send something beautiful to listen to as we started our days. *'Whatever else is going on, the Lord God reigns. Alleluia.'* She attached a link to a worship track from Hillsong called *Agnus Dei/ King of Kings*. The lyrics read:

Alleluia, Alleluia
For the Lord God Almighty reigns
Alleluia, Alleluia
For the Lord God Almighty reigns
Alleluia
Holy, Holy

Are You Lord God Almighty
Worthy is the Lamb
Worthy is the Lamb
You are Holy, Holy
Are You Lord God Almighty
Worthy is the Lamb
Worthy is the Lamb
Amen
In the darkness we were waiting
Without hope, without light
'Til from heaven You came running
There was mercy in Your eyes
To fulfill the law and prophets
To a virgin came the word
From a throne of endless glory
To a cradle in the dirt
Praise the Father, praise the Son
Praise the Spirit, three in one
God of glory, Majesty
Praise forever to the King of kings
To reveal the Kingdom coming
And to reconcile the lost
To redeem the whole creation
You did not despise the cross
For even in Your suffering
You saw to the other side
Knowing this was our salvation
Jesus for our sake You died
Praise the Father, praise the Son

And praise the Spirit, three in one
God of glory, Majesty
Praise forever to the King of kings
And the morning that You rose
All of heaven held its breath
'Til that stone was moved for good
For the Lamb had conquered death
And the dead rose from their tombs
And the angels stood in awe
For the souls of all who'd come
To the Father are restored
And the church of Christ was born
Then the Spirit lit the flame
Now this gospel truth of old
Shall not kneel, shall not faint
By His blood and in His name
In His freedom I am free
For the love of Jesus Christ
Who Has resurrected me
Praise the Father, praise the Son
Praise the Spirit, three in one
God of glory, Majesty
And praise forever to the King of kings
Praise the Father, praise the Son
Praise the Spirit, three in one
God of glory, Majesty
Praise forever to the King of kings
Praise forever to the King of kings
We praise forever to the King of kings [12]

I listened to the track that I had never heard before knowing that my friend did not know anything about what had happened in the night.

I sobbed.

THE FOLLOWING Sunday I went to church as usual. I was not preaching that week and we had organised the lectionary readings a couple of months before. I was astounded to learn that the gospel reading was John 1: 29-42 about John the Baptist seeing Jesus in the desert saying, '*Here is the Lamb of God who takes away the sin of the world!* ' My colleague, Lisa, preached a great sermon on the Lamb of God without any knowledge of what I had experienced only a few days earlier.

While God still whispers in the silence, I am relieved that at times He shouts and His words are unmistakable.

17

WORKING FROM REST

I *don't believe in any religion apart from doing the will of God.'*

Catherine Booth

'It is natural to talk about the benefits of rest from work, but it is difficult to see how we put into practice working from rest.

The Ambassador

Reflecting on my earlier dream about the Seal of the Lamb, and the later confirmations about the importance of Agnus Dei, I recognised that the seal is significant in my understanding of being an ambassador. It reminds me that Jesus has the authority to set the captives free but He also gives it to us to carry on His behalf and represent Him in the world. While I had lots to ponder, I was still left with an unpleasant migraine. Thankfully it only lasted one full day and I had no sickness with it, but it still made me miserable. When was this ever going to end? I didn't believe that this was my cross to bear, or the thorn in my side. My discomfort and frustration sent me back to my two-way journaling to have it out with God. I wrote:

- 'What about the migraines Lord, do I really have to put up with them?'

'This is still part of the journey and it's not just for you. This is for lots of people. Because I know that you can hold this and will write about it, it is for others' sake that I allow this. Had you been healed the first time you prayed you would not have learned and discovered what you have. But don't misunderstand this Mandy, I'm not forcing these on you and I'm not preventing your healing. I'm cramming as much learning in until you take them down yourself and can do the same for others. I want your suffering to end, but I want it to end for others too and you have a part to play in this. What you learn you will teach others and then the darkness will be very afraid of you.

Take the longer view – I know it already feels far too long – but come up higher. See the perspective from heavenly places. You will carry the hard-won revelation to set the captives free. The word of your testimony becomes the seed that grows and blossoms into others' freedom. It is suffering - but it is not without purpose.

You will be free of migraines but not yet. When you learn what you need to, then you will bless others with their freedom.'

- 'That sounds great Lord, but this is still horrible! How do I cope in the meantime?'

'You spend time on The Beach with Me. Without that you will become angry and you will start to question My goodness and My love for you. I am not bringing these migraines to you, but I am redeeming them in the longer term, intermingling My love and purposes for you with them, not for you only, but for others. If you stay away from The Beach, you miss My love for you.

You think you have to have it all figured out- all theologically correct, when in fact, I just want you to let Me love you. I just want you to rest and receive from Me and let Me renew your heart.

I have taught you so much on The Beach, don't neglect the lessons. Come and receive My love.'

Although it is still a disappointment that I haven't been miraculously healed, I begrudgingly accept that God is probably right. I feel a sense of resonance within as the witness of the Spirit confirms what has been written in my journal. I will

continue to pursue God and all He has for me with
the faith that one day, I will be healed. Knowing how
awful this chronic condition is and talking to other
sufferers, I do see the wisdom in God ensuring that
my healing is not for me alone. Until then I need
patience, and that is something I have in short
supply. I am finding this refining process a challenge, but probably a necessary one.

God's direction to go back to The Beach to
remember His goodness also strikes a chord in me.
How easy it is to get into a cycle of complaint and
grumbling, even when God has done and continues
to do amazing things. It reminds me of the Israelites
trekking through the desert moaning and groaning
about how they wished they were back in Egypt
after everything God had done for them. We have
short memories when it comes to God's goodness,
and incredibly long ones when it comes to our own
disappointments.

After this conversation, I took on what had been
said to me and went back to The Beach. I got into
bed, put my earplugs in, and relaxed, letting the
sound of the sea take me to that secret place of
encounter. In my garden I have a double-pod swing
chair which I absolutely love. When the Summer is
here, I enjoy sitting in the chair, stretching out and
gently swinging as I read a book. This time, when I
went to The Beach I saw just this kind of double-pod
chair standing in the sand and Abba inviting me to

sit with Him. It wasn't for some instruction, it was just to keep Him company.

It wasn't long before the gentle movement of the swing-chair and His comforting presence made me feel relaxed. I put a cushion in His lap and rested the side of my head on it as I looked out to the sea with the waves breaking on the shore. Abba welcomed me snuggling down and getting comfortable and His big hand started to gently stroke my head. I was completely relaxed and He seemed to be too. There was no awkward silence, just a deep peace. I didn't have to say anything, and He remained quiet too. I listened to Him breathing as well as the rhythm of the waves. It brought a sense of completeness to me that I wanted to last for ever. Then, unsurprisingly, I fell asleep in my imagination and in my bed at home. It was a beautiful experience.

My reflections on what had been said and the swing-chair on The Beach brought me to consider the place of rest in our lives. Dr. Caroline Leaf, speaking as a person of faith as well as a cognitive neuroscientist, explains how instructions such as 'Be still and know that I am God'[1] link with key scientific concepts in her field of understanding. She writes:

'*When we direct our rest by introspection, self-reflection, and prayer; when we catch our thoughts; when we memorize and quote Scripture; and when we develop our mind intellectually, we enhance the default mode network (DMN) that improves brain function and mental, physical, and spiritual health.'* [2]...*'When our brain enters the rest circuit, we don't actually rest; we move into a highly intelligent, self-reflective, directed state. And the more often we go there, the more we get in touch with the deep, spiritual part of who we are.'* [3]

When we activate this default mode network, Dr. Leaf argues that the effect is almost like having a Sabbath in the brain which stops the conscious busyness of work. It acts like a mental rebooting process giving us improved perspective. It activates to an even higher level when a person is daydreaming, letting their mind wander, focusing inward and tuning out the outside world.[4] It helps us to understand how using our imagination with God, whether it's the Ignatian Spiritual Exercises or simply lying in a swing-chair with Abba, can be a source of learning, rest, and encounter. It also explains how flow states, such as those I was experiencing in two-way journaling, can enrich our connection with the God who dwells deep within us.

It is natural to talk about the benefits of rest from work, but it is difficult to see how we put into practice working from rest. It is not something that I see around me and it hasn't been something that I have practiced myself. Looking back at my working life, I can seen periods of over-work. I have started early and finished late and done the same thing the next day and the day after, until I am exhausted. There is always more to do, but some of our tendency to over-work is our fault. The truth is that we often say 'yes' when we should be saying 'no' and we deprive others of their responsibility by taking it off of them and over-functioning on their behalf. When we are conscientious and believe in what we are doing we can create our own work. We say it's because we care and it matters, but at times it may be because we have impaired boundaries and too much of our identity is tied up in what we do, so it's threatening to our core if we fail to live up to our, or others' expectations.

I remember working in an outreach centre in London run by the Salvation Army when I was in my early twenties. It was only a temporary job working on the administrative side. Next to an open office, there was a drop-in centre for people who were homeless. One day I was typing away and I heard this woman behind me shout accusingly at me:

"How dare you say you're a Christian. There's no food in this place!"

I was shocked because the drop-in centre was just for tea and coffee and there were other facilities that offered meals. In the absence of anyone else being available I sheepishly went to the fridge and found some bread and cheese for this woman. I was told later the woman was a drug user and was looking to have something in her stomach before she used, which explained the way she acted towards me.

I remember this so well all these years later because I had been hooked in to comply to this woman's demands with the accusation that I was a bad Christian if I didn't. I wonder how much of our Christian activity is influenced by guilt, shame, and fear? There are also natural challenges in following a sinless Saviour. We may interpret Jesus' command to take up our cross as meaning that we pick up every cross going, even those that don't belong to us. His call to forgive transgressions may cause us to rush to cover over every sin with love[5] without first properly acknowledging the truth for others and ourselves. Church Leaders are particularly vulnerable to forming shiny personas which mask oppressive slave-drivers within, because we carry so many projected ideals of what it means to be a spiritual leader. When we don't challenge these false images, they shape expectations in the community and create stress and disappointment when the hopes of that same community are inevitably frustrated. Compared with the romanticized, and often misremembered, standard set by a beloved previous minister in the 1950s, today's leaders regularly come up short. The response to this occupational hazard is not to work harder and longer but to inhabit our grounded and authentic humanity and be humble and honest enough to let people see it.

Over-work is a common problem for Christian Leaders and those who volunteer in the Church. It is as if no other calling is as important as ministry and therefore the sacrifices that we, our family and social networks make, are sanctified because we're 'working for the kingdom.' I've noticed that when Clergy Chapters get together there is almost a contest over who is most busy, who is the most tired, and who has the greatest number of people coming to their church. It's straight out of the first disciples' playbook. It is as if God is going to award a medal for whomever suffers the most, but there's only one prize so His children must compete to prove their faithfulness.

These workaholic tendencies seem to increase when the Church is facing decline. Many congregations have aged and are dwindling, which creates more challenges. In the Church of England, these challenges might include finding someone to step up to be the Churchwarden or Treasurer, finding the funds to repair a crumbling ancient building, or facing pastoral re-organisations where resources are shared over a wider area. Memories of large, robed choirs or Sunday Schools that were bursting at the seams are remembered as the golden age that is now gone. Leaders, both lay and ordained, are sent out to stir up faith, look at more community engagement, and bring hope to congregations that have been faithful but are often tired and worn out themselves by keeping everything going. This is not the only image of the modern church, but it is a recognisable one in many areas.

All but the big, well-resourced churches (and even some of those) struggle with finding volunteers to take on roles, and attendance patterns vary more than they used to. The changes to our lifestyle, working practices and Sunday trading laws all make a difference, as does the decline in the number of those who publicly declare themselves Christians. National denominational structures attempt to encourage congregations everywhere by casting their visions and strategies, publicising campaigns, and calling everyone to get on board and on message to keep the faith and stop the decline. I have often heard the prayer, attributed to Teresa of Ávila, being used as both carrot and stick to encourage more working for the kingdom.

"Christ has no body now but yours. No hands, no feet on earth but yours. Yours are the eyes through which he looks compassion on this world. Yours are the feet with which he walks to do good. Yours are the hands through which he blesses all the world. Yours are the hands, yours are the feet, yours are the eyes, you are his body. Christ has no body now on earth but yours."

Even prayers of past Saints can add unhelpful pressure to declining congregations who already feel overstretched and exhausted.

Jeremy Myers, in his book *The Death and Resur-*

rection of the Church calls for a reality check about our own values, and to be ruthlessly honest about the Church's departure from kingdom values. He argues that much of our angst is really about our own need to control and cling to past glories. He is scathing about copying the world in its methods of consumption and entertainment in the hope that people might be 'unaware when we throw the gospel into their cart as well,'[6] reminding his readers that the world notices these attempts to copy and is not impressed. It is clear to the world that the methods and message do not mix. The solution is to recognise the difference and to re-engage with kingdom thinking and values. This means letting go of the measuring tools that the world uses to assess 'success' because the kingdom has a different focus. As Heidi Baker reminds us in *Learning to Love*, this is loving God and loving the one in front of us.[7] Kingdom life isn't always about the big and shiny and numerous. It's found in the small, the hidden, and the everyday. It's one heart at a time, one sheep, one coin, and two lost sons.

Martyn Percy's book *The Humble Church* critiques how the modern church is functioning, claiming we have lost our way. It is not that numbers are irrelevant, but that our focus and priorities should be different. He argues:

'The church needs a complete restart if it seeks to be revitalized. The question is not 'how can we get more

people into church?' but rather, 'how can we get more
people from church to love and serve the world, as Christ
would have us do? Instead of trying to refill the church,
start from a different premise: that if we put God and the
needs of the world before the church, the growth that
many so desperately crave, plan for and try and resource
may actually come. But if we put the needs of the church
first, we shall continue to empty.' [8]

Jeremy Myers also brings us back to the model of
Jesus, asking the question:

'So what drew people to Jesus? It was His love and
acceptance, His identification with their pain, and His
willingness to go where they were and be with them.
Such things are central to the incarnation of Jesus.' [9]

Re-focusing on the life of Jesus seems an obvious
thing to say but it is amazing how quickly we can
drift to other models that have nothing to do with
kingdom values. They may seem plausible because
the world tells us how we become a success and
what that looks like, but I'm not sure that worldly
success is a top priority in the kingdom. It's much
more about faithfulness than it is about growth,
numbers, power, and prestige. Until we recognise
this and alter the direction of our words and actions,
we are likely to keep going down the wrong path and
exhausting ourselves in the process.

During my two-way journaling, I had a prophetic
word about the new season, and I bravely shared it
in a diocesan residential conference. As always, I

offered it open-handedly, inviting the Body of Christ to weigh it up and to let it fall to the ground if it did not resonate with them. This was not the response, however. Instead, people were encouraged to the point that several of my colleagues took copies of it and said how they felt the witness of the Spirit within them as it was said. This word is simple, but it narrows our view. It is:

"What do people need? Do they need more of you or more of Me? Where does their help come from? What makes the difference? What do I call you to and where do I call you?

Recalibration is the word for this season, a reordering, a re-orientation of life with me at the centre. Whenever anything else takes the centre, it becomes an idol. It shifts you away from my priorities.

Preach me. That's all." [10]

We see this at work in places like Mozambique. The Bakers have children as young as six praying for deaf ears and blind eyes to open and it happens. These children do not have three years of theological training, they just know what God offers.[11] Heidi Baker writes:

'It takes courage to go, but it can take more courage to let go. To let go of the reins that you have been holding on to. Let go of your way, let go of being the answer.' [12]

If there is a message for the modern church to learn it is this: Too often we are trying to be the answer instead of just following the leader. So much of our angst about church growth is because we are still thinking it's about us and what we do or don't do. "If only we could get the right minister or youth worker then we'd fill the church." "What we need is different music, or to take out the pews." "If we do those things then we will reverse decline, grow and flourish." But this is not what Jesus says. When I was thinking about this, God reminded me of a short parable in Mark 4:

[Jesus] also said, 'This is what the kingdom of God is like. A man scatters seed on the ground. Night and day, whether he sleeps or gets up, the seed sprouts and grows, though he does not know how. All by itself, the soil produces corn – first the stalk, then the ear, then the full grain in the ear. As soon as the corn is ripe, he puts the sickle to it because the harvest has come.' [13]

What strikes me about this story is the fact that all the man does is scatter the seed. The rest is up to the soil and the seed itself. Jesus emphasises this by drawing attention to the fact that, whether the man 'sleeps or gets up' is irrelevant because 'all by itself' the seed in the soil creates a harvest. This parable is a challenge to all over-active ministries where we wear ourselves out for the sake of the Gospel and encourage others to do the same.

This way of thinking requires a radical spiritual change because we are still trying to save the church by our own hand. We have gone about it the wrong way. Instead of seeking the kingdom and letting

Jesus build His church, we work hard at all manner of strategies and programmes and invite Jesus to bless *our* works. Working from rest is like getting out of the way so that God can be and do what God is and does.

Returning to the prophetic word that I shared at the conference, when we make something other than Jesus the centre of our worshipping life, it becomes an idol. Because there is no kingdom life in an idol, we must animate it by putting energy and effort into it to give it the appearance of vitality. Compare this with Jesus' promises of giving life in all its fullness [14] and that living waters will flow from within all who believe in Him.[15] Jesus gives us abundant life but in one of the Bible's paradoxical statements, it is coupled with learning to die. Jesus says:

'Very truly I tell you, unless a kernel of wheat falls to the ground and dies, it remains only a single seed. But if it dies, it produces many seeds. Anyone who loves their life will lose it, while anyone who hates their life in this world will keep it for eternal life.' [16]

Jesus is using the hyperbole common in the rhetoric of the time, but we can see that there is something fruitful about surrendering to God. We learn to die to self and let Him work within us, rather than clinging to our ego, filling our lives with all we want and many distractions. This is illustrated by a story about the Desert Fathers who were early Christian monks, living in Egypt in the third century.

A brother went to Abba Moses to ask for a word of advice on living the monastic life. Abba Moses told him:

'Go, sit in your cell and your cell will teach you everything.'

Some believe that living in monastic communities is a form of escapism, but it is, in fact, the opposite. This is because confronting our own egos and having no diversion from fellow residents who annoy us as much as we surely irritate them, brings us face to face with our own self and our need to control, defend, and promote ourselves. We are in a crucible for transformation, bringing the impurities visibly to the surface. I remember, some years ago, hearing a Mother Abbess of a community speaking fondly of an older nun who had just come to live with them. She said: "We can enjoy her sanctity without having had to endure her sanctification."

Most of us today do not live as hermits or part of a religious community, but when we make time to be alone with God, without rushing off into distractions or 'works' for Him, we too can come into that place for refining and intimacy.

Working from rest is recognising that it's not about us, it's about Jesus and His kingdom. We don't have to force anything or be the answer - because Jesus is. When we preach Him, and point to Him in all we do, it takes the pressure off us. We become aware of the idols that have taken Jesus' place and we can surrender them. They are in the way of *The Way*.[17] When the Church recalibrates everything we do to Jesus, then others see Him, not our poor and distorted images. Instead, we teach and model the direct relationship with Him, showing there's no longer a veil in the Temple, we can all have access to Him.[18] What a relief it is that we can work from rest knowing that Jesus is the one that everyone needs and He's already loving the one in front of us.

Sometimes we just need to get out of the way.

18

LIVING INSIDE OUT FOR OTHERS

'N o power on earth or in hell can conquer the Spirit of God in a human spirit.'

Oswald Chambers

'Living the kingdom is not a consumer model. It does not correspond to the world's standards because it uses a different measure.'

The Ambassador

There is a story that, in 1908, William Booth, the Co-Founder of the Salvation Army, sent a Christmas message to Salvationists around the world. Communication was by telegraph in those days and every word had to be paid for. As times were financially tough for the Salvation Army, he sent just one word on it: 'Others'. He hoped that this single focus would encourage the mission of their movement to even greater service.[1]

This is a good reminder for all of us that our life with God isn't just about us. Neither is it just about our church or our local community. It is about everyone, everywhere. When I wrote about my experiences on *The Beach* getting to know Father, Son and Holy Spirit, it was enriching to my faith, my identity, and my well-being. God has reminded me to come back to this secret place often, to be with Him, receive from Him and learn to love and accept love. It was, and continues to be, a wonderful, life-giving, and affirming experience. Through it, I have discovered the unconditional love of God that brings me peace, joy, and a sense of completeness. I cannot imagine life without experiencing the love and delight of beach life. It has changed me, settled me, healed many wounds, and helped me to grow downwards into the freedom of being a child of God.

I believe that these benefits are a gift for everyone who learns to spend time in their secret place with God, whether it's on a beach, or in a forest, or on a mountain top. When we know that we are a loved child of God and that nothing can shake this, it shows up in our life. Peace replaces anxiety. We feel a sense of freedom and we can let go of the things we carry. It gives us a quality that can be seen in our lives, just like we can recognise when people are in love. Without experiencing the First Love of God, faith can become hard work and Christian service demanding. We become slaves to the task and easily exhausted and discouraged. What a difference it makes if we can spend time with God, fill up with His presence and be empowered with His energy for the purposes He calls us to.

Having a loving relationship with the Holy Trinity is a foundational layer of our experience with God, but it is not the whole story. If we only stay in our secret place with God, it becomes solely about us, our experiences, our feelings, our well-being, and our spiritual growth. We may be learning to love God and receive love, but love is always meant to be shared and passed on, not hoarded.

Sadly, the belief that my relationship with God is just about me is an assumption to which those of us in the Western world are particularly prone. Following Jesus may have been a personal decision, but it's not meant to be a solitary journey. We are made for community as the Trinity models for us. Randolph Richards and Brandon O'Brien write:

'This cultural assumption about the supremacy of me is the one to which we Westerners are perhaps blindest.' [2]

This tunnel vision also affects how we read the Bible and how we see Jesus. Richard Horsley writes:

'...projecting a modern Western assumption onto ancient society, we think of Jesus as an individual figure independent of the social relations in which he was

embedded. And we think of Jesus as having dealt mainly with other individuals, not with social groups and political institutions.' [3]

If we don't take in the bigger, connected picture then, when we read the Bible, we become the centre of our own analysis. Following Jesus then becomes less about taking up our cross and more about coming to Him so He'll make our lives better.[4] Churches often hop on the cultural bandwagon to try to answer the *what's in it for me?* question. Martyn Percy wryly offers an analysis of what seeing faith in these consumer terms might look like:

'It offers comfort, bolsters self-esteem, helps solve problems, and lubricates interpersonal relationships by encouraging people to do good, feel good, and keep God at arm's length...its thrust is personal happiness and helping people treat each other nicely.' [5]

The consumer model majors on the important role of marketing. When companies want to sell a product, they outline the benefits and know that advertising is key. Words and images create a brand and, with some clever psycholinguistics, people will connect with that vision and buy in to it by purchasing the product. As the Church increasingly has a media presence, we are encouraged to think about our 'customers', with our websites and social media posts becoming our shop window to sell our particular brand of church. I am all for a modern looking church with up-to-date methods of expressing community life but, when the message becomes about us and our comfort, we have drifted off course. We also run into difficulties if we seek to grow a church that is based on a consumer model. People have different preferences and it's exhausting trying to provide for every age group and demographic and to be all things to all people.

It is hard to hear that a teenager is no longer coming because there's nothing *for them* now. Or to hear someone has stopped attending Sunday Worship because *they're not getting anything out of it.* While this is disappointing, it is also real. We can all be opinionated about what we like and what we don't, even if it's more about style than substance. Consumerism affects all ages and we bring it into our church life and ministry planning.

We are called to proclaim the gospel afresh in each generation,[6] but that doesn't always happen, especially when it doesn't suit *our* preferences. Tradition can be beautiful and life-giving, providing ancient paths for people to journey towards God. It can also feel like *peer pressure from dead people*. When I first heard that comment, it made me laugh but it isn't really a laughing matter if tradition makes us inflexible, inward-looking, and inhospitable to other people. Although it's hard for us to admit it, when we have a personal investment in things staying just as we like them, we function like the stopper in the bottle. Over time, our communal life becomes stale and stagnant because there is no freshness or renewal. It has been my observation that at the root of many church divisions is the belief that *we* are the most important customers who should be catered for before others and that never bodes well for the life, message, outreach, and vitality of the local church.

Tying our wagon to consumerism creates a twofold problem. First, it requires us to compete with other service providers who are usually better resourced than us and more attractive to consumers. Secondly, and more importantly, it has little to do with the Gospel of Christ. And there should be a difference, because, as we considered earlier, our identity as citizens of the kingdom, makes us different. Drawing together some of the themes in this book, we begin to see what it might look like in practice to inhabit our role as citizens and ambassadors.

If we are to speak on behalf of the kingdom as its representatives, we must also exemplify its practices and values. This means thinking kingdom thoughts and upholding kingdom standards. We join in with God's Mission, rather than asking Him to bless our own programmes. We have access to His heart and His purposes revealed in the life of Jesus, and we see this fulfilled through all that was accomplished by the cross. We are empowered by the Holy Spirit to represent Him in the world, listening for, and responding to, His voice, not just in the Bible but within our spirits too. We recognise we are in union with Him; He is God-with-us and, therefore, we have access to all the resources of the kingdom through Him. He has given us His seal of authority to carry on His work, to preach the good news to the poor, to set the captives free, proclaiming the Lord's favour for all His people. We get to enjoy what He has already accomplished and take it further by applying it to our context in partnership with Him.

There are no half-measures because we are asked for our whole hearts, minds, bodies and spirits. Suffering is part of the cost of discipleship and if we're looking for a comfortable ride - then this isn't it. When the kingdom really takes hold of us, it turns our lives upside down. It can dislocate us from our surroundings, shining a spotlight on where the new culture clashes with the old. What we thought was valuable in life is shown to be the reverse, and what we previously looked down on is honoured. It provides a nagging tug on our spirits, convicting us when we are selfish and looking only to our own interests. For those of us who always want to believe the best about ourselves, thinking our motives are pure, it can become a thorn in our side.

It is a whole new way of seeing and being, often going against societal norms and the grain of human nature. Others may think we are naïve, foolish, and stupid. They may laugh at us and ridicule us. For some it will be worse. It may even cost us our lives as it has others before us. However, we cannot go back. When the love of God becomes real to us in greater measure it changes us. We have tasted kingdom life and freedom and we cannot return to believing what we did before, knowing what we know now. It would be returning to the less and to the artificial. Instead, we must go deeper in.

When we cannot give up being citizens from another homeland, we must learn to live with that dislocation within us, knowing that one day, we will return home. For the time being, however, we are advocates and ambassadors for God's reign on earth, seeing His glorious kingdom break through, 'on earth as in heaven' and bringing the reality of God's love and power to those around us.

Living the kingdom is not a consumer model. It does not correspond to the world's standards because it uses a different measure. The spiritual writer and mystic, Henri Nouwen, writes:

'Too often I looked at being relevant, popular, and powerful as ingredients of an effective ministry. The truth, however, is that these are not vocations but temptations.' [7]

There have been times throughout church history when the glitter of Empire held sway over the authentic nature of the kingdom. In the first couple of centuries, the Jesus movement developed and grew, particularly under persecution by various Roman Emperors. Then a shift came when Emperor

Constantine converted to Christianity. After defeating his enemies under the sign of the cross, he declared the Christian faith the official religion of the Roman Empire. Jeremy Myers writes:

'Almost overnight, Christianity became rich, powerful, and prominent. It also became a tool of the Empire. The leaders of Christianity blessed the Empire's wars, approved the Empire's laws, and installed the Empire's rulers. In exchange, the Empire gave land, money, and buildings to the church, which only increased the church's power, influence, fame and worldly glory.' [8]

After this, it was difficult for Kingdom people to provide the social critique of the Empire's values. The Church had now been enlisted to support and legitimise them.

The Church is, therefore, not the same as the kingdom and can even be at odds with it. Jesus tells the disciples to seek *first* His kingdom[9] and *He* will be the one who builds the Church.[10] The Pastor, Pete Carter, reflects on the call by asking himself,

'Did I have a 'Kingdom – first mindset' or a Church – first mindset?...To place the kingdom before the Church does not reduce the Church in any way. Rather is sets it in a healthy context within which it can grow and develop.' [11]

Kingdom people are those who know what, and whom, they represent. It is not enough for it to be about us and our preferences. When a teacher of the law asks Jesus what the most important commandment is, He replies with the accepted answer of the *Shema,* a command to love God with all one's heart, soul, mind and strength.[12] To this, however, He adds the second commandment which is to love one's neighbour as oneself.[13] Both are in the Hebrew Scriptures but Jesus puts them together.[14] On the night before He dies, He says to His disciples at supper:

'My command is this: love each other as I have loved you. Greater love has no one than this: to lay down one's life for one's friends.' [15]

Not only has Jesus linked love of neighbour with the love of God, but He is now saying *'as I have loved you.'* He becomes the pattern for what that looks like and what lengths that love will go to. It is not enough to love God alone. It is now part of our devotion to God that we will love our neighbours who are made in His image, and we are to love in a way that may require us to lay our lives down for them. We cannot separate our worship of God from our responsibility and practice to love one another, and not just our friends and family.

Jesus calls Israel to a renewal of community. Part of this rebirth requires the people to address their own shortcomings. They are called to go through the narrow gate,[16] challenging the easy, unimpeded way of their assumed superiority and favour. To live truly as the people of God requires them to repent, turning away from wrong thinking and learning to

see things differently. Some of these new lessons are
particularly hard for an oppressed people, especially
the command to love one's enemies. We see this
teaching in action when Jesus makes a hated Samar-
itan the hero of a Jewish story and commends the
faith of a Roman occupier. We also see how Jesus
praises a sex worker's act of anointing His feet and
head, when such hospitality was not offered by His
religious host. He also makes a woman who had
been delivered from demons the first witness and
herald of His resurrection.[17] Again and again, He
blurs the boundaries of what is considered right and
holy. And why? Because He's calling the new Israel
to go beyond these boundaries, to see how God sees
and to love as God loves. This is never meant to be a
life in isolation. This is a new community of love
that reflects the kingdom and the model that its king
has set.

Love is front and centre in the ministry of Jesus
and the Early Church understood that and carried it
on. Whether it is Paul's poem on love in 1
Corinthians 13 that we often hear at weddings, or
John the Apostle's beautiful chapter calling us to
love one another because love comes from God,[18] we
cannot separate the expression of our faith from the
practice of loving others. What Jesus proclaims in
Luke 4, that we call His *Nazareth Manifesto,* is still
central today and good news to those who receive it.
Heidi Baker writes:

'We run into the darkness looking for good news because it is the power of God that gives the world hope. We don't apologise for seeking and valuing God's power, because without it love is incomplete and ineffectual. Love is not powerless.' [19]

The Bakers explain the growth of their organisation in Mozambique as due to marriage of love and power. It hasn't been through methods, programmes or techniques but knowing how to humble themselves before God.[20] They say:

'God is calling us to lay down spiritually – to let Him love us until we are full of Him, full of His love and His life. And so we must fight, not to make a temple but to become His temple. To become a resting place for His beautiful, holy habitation. To be fully possessed by the glory of the Lord. He is calling us not to run harder, but to lay down.'

This is a counter-cultural message for most of us in the Western church, but it chimes with the message of the kingdom.

As I look back to the prophetic word from 24.1.21, I have been evaluating how much I have learned in writing this book. The union we have with God-with-us can never be overstated. Although we might not feel that deep connection now, it is there for us to discover, to learn from, and to delight in. The kingdom is established when we work in partnership with the God who has already accomplished everything we need through the cross. We are invited to join Him in proclaiming His mission to the world and see His reign break into our dimension, in big and small ways. He is looking for those willing to carry the Lamb of God's seal and to serve the release papers so the captives can be set free. He has done what is necessary but He's waiting for the Church to discover the authority we have been given.

Instead, there are many of us in the Church who have drifted away from the call to be an outpost of the counter-cultural kingdom. We have wrongly equated faithfulness with worldly success and laboured to build the Church instead of seeking the kingdom and letting Jesus build the Church. We have exhausted our people with an emphasis on works rather than grace, and on us rather than God. Our anxiety about the future shows we have not learned the principle that, in dying to ourselves, we will live. Many dead works are on life-support, when in fact, somebody, or anybody, with courage and prophetic truth should pull the plug. It is only then we will discover true resurrection life.

Re-orientating ourselves to kingdom life means letting go of our need to control. It means being brave to do less and let some things die. It requires the radical repentance of changing our minds, recognising that we have not sought the kingdom, but have been swayed by the glitter of Empire and the power and glory that is not rooted in the love of others.

When we face the reality that we cannot save ourselves and we have come to the end of our resources, that is the time to re-focus. We are ready to be found by Him. It is like the prodigal's story. We are at the edge of our village coming home, but there are still temptations to try to control what happens next, to be independent, planning to do our own thing. It is at this point that we have an opportunity to lay down our schemes and plans and accept the utter love and grace of God. Abba is waiting with His arms out. He's not interested in what we have or haven't done, He just wants us home and to renounce that independence that drew us away from Him in the first place. When we are in His arms, we re-discover who we are and we see all our striving for what it is. We remember our family values and the identity and the love we have been given and, in turn, the call to represent the family in the world.

Kingdom people don't have to have everything figured out and planned for because we are constantly listening for, and guided by, our king's voice. His Spirit leads us to represent Him wherever He calls. He may direct us to go a different way because of His kingdom purposes. He sets us up with 'Divine appointments' and He calls us to stop for the one, the hidden and forgotten, rather than just head for the big, the popular, and the shiny. Following Him requires greater flexibility and spontaneity. This is a terrifying prospect for those of us who live by plans, strategies and clearly marked objectives, but we must go when He says go, and let go, when He tells us to. We know that wherever He calls us, He goes too, and we are never separated from His love.

Living inside-out means recognising the treasure He has put within us. We have access to all His resources and when we practise humility, saying 'not our will but Yours', He begins to shine through us more. The union we have is expressed in what we do and how we are. We are entrusted to carry more of His glory and as people who are in love, it will be seen. God looks for those of us who will carry His light and know that the all-surpassing power is from Him and not from us.[21] Heidi Baker writes:

'Our power is in the cross of Jesus and nowhere else. So we invade the darkness with the Word of the Lord and Blood of the Lamb.' [22]

We are ambassadors for the kingdom, proclaiming the finished work of our king and His love for all the world. When the people of God arise as the light of the world, we will have re-discovered our vocation, and pushed back the darkness, to advance the kingdom of our God.

EPILOGUE - THE ROPE SWING AT THE
END OF THE BRIDGE

'*L*ive in the kingdom of God in such a way that it provokes questions for which the gospel is the answer.'

Lesslie Newbigin

'*How do 'process and risk', 'knowledge and mystery', 'experience and faith', all work together? What does it mean to have life in all its fullness given to us by the Spirit, but to be willing to die to oneself to have it? It seems to me that this is a juxtaposition of opposites and yet, when I saw the rope swing next to the end of the bridge in my imagination, I realise this one image encapsulates it all.*'

The Ambassador

It has been an interesting journey. It has been part reflection, part formation and reformation, and part education and training. It has involved a shift within me and in my understanding of what the Church is for and what I, as a minister of the Gospel, am called to do and be. It has brought greater focus and freedom. I have discovered that much of what I *thought* I had to take on to build the Church in our area, I have, instead, to release and it's a blessing to do so. I am still a minister in the Church of God, but I see this in terms of seeking the kingdom first.

It has also changed my perception of leadership. I now want to make more space for God to lead, to empower, and to speak. We are His ambassadors, so although we represent Him, everything we do points to Him not to us. We get out of the way so He can be seen more clearly.

What this looks like in practice is making more space for God to arise in our consciousness. He is there already, whether we are aware of Him or not, but creating more space for listening and responding to Him actively changes our focus so we can see Him at work and He never disappoints.

A typical church service at St. George's has a liturgy, a set number of hymns or songs, collective prayers and an opportunity to receive the bread and wine in Holy Communion. We are not on the cutting edge of modern worship. Nor are we trying to be on brand for any other church 'type'. As a small, rural community, we take a middle way in the Church of England, avoiding the ends of the spectrum but being open to where God is leading us. Yet, in recent months, we have noticed a quality of quiet and an atmosphere of peace growing. We are actively making more time and space to reflect and taking more risks in saying what we hear from God.

None of this is rocket science. It's the kind of thing my colleagues and their congregations are doing up and down the land, in big cathedrals and tiny chapels, and everything in between. We are not special or unique in this way. However, we are on a journey, moving on from where we were, going deeper in our understanding and devotion, and raising our expectations of God among us.

I am privileged to be part of a church family that has a history of faithful prayer, and this legacy is felt in the building, imprinting something holy and sacred in its very stones. It creates a 'thin' place for heaven to break through. People comment on the peace and the beautiful atmosphere, whether they come to sit in an empty church or join us for Sunday worship. It is usual for people to weep while not knowing why they are doing so. Even some men who are not necessarily given to the easy expression of their emotions have found themselves moved. This is drawing people back, not because we are relevant or offering resources for a modern lifestyle, but because there is something else, something numinous, which is beyond what we can muster up ourselves. This is not about 'blowing our own trumpet' but delighting in the presence of God among us. It's also just the beginning.

God calls us to go out. We are never meant to remain in holy huddles. Much of Jesus' ministry happens out in the fields, along the roads, in people's homes and in the public places in the community. Comparatively little happens in the synagogue or temple. Often, Jesus has significant encounters on the way to somewhere else, but He stops for the one. He doesn't have a tightly planned schedule enslaved to the clock and He takes Himself off alone when He needs to re-balance His energies and speak with Abba. We know that He is heading to Jerusalem and that there is a plan and purpose in play, but along the way He stops for others, or is stopped by them, with His mercy always leading the way.

Jesus also sends His followers out on mission trips. The twelve and seventy-two are not expected to stay in a building together to express their faith.[1] They are to take the message and practice of the kingdom out to where the people are. They are given power and authority and told to drive out demons, cure diseases, proclaim the Kingdom of God, and even to raise the dead.[2] This is about kingdom power breaking into our dimension and bringing transformation. The disciples become mobile portals of the kingdom.

This makes sense when we go back to Chapter one and consider the words Jesus says in Luke 17: 21 about the kingdom being within us. Jesus exemplifies everything about the nature of the kingdom. He is the king and all power and authority comes from Him. It therefore makes sense that if the king lives within us then we carry the kingdom inside of us wherever we go. We have all the resources of heaven within us waiting to be released. What stops the release is the flotsam and jetsam of our lives that dam up the flow.

This is why keeping short accounts with God is necessary. Many of us may feel broken by what seems like the 'slings and arrows of outrageous fortune.'[3] Part of this journey is recognising that we don't have to stay fractured and fragmented. It's not our identity as children of God and He can heal us. He then sends us out with a testimony of His love and grace to share His goodness with others. This journey may be personal, but it's never a solitary pilgrimage. We are made for community, generosity, and hospitality so that others may enjoy His light and love.

It was early morning and in my imagination I saw the bridge that I had been building as I walked along it. There were no more bricks and I was stranded in mid-air. What could I do? I could turn around and go back the way I came in the hope that more bricks would materialise, or I could find another route. Perhaps I'd gone the wrong way and the bridge should have taken me to solid ground by now had I built it in the right direction. I looked ahead and I could see blue sky and sunshine but no land on the horizon. What I saw however, was a rope swing where the bridge ended. It was a big, thick rope with a knot on its end, but I couldn't see where it was suspended from. It hung there, without explanation or instruction. I felt intrigued as well as mildly anxious.

This reminded me of Henri Nouwen's passion for the circus and in particular, the trapeze artists. The *Flying Rodleighs* were a South-African troupe who Nouwen loved to watch and to gain spiritual insights from. He came to understand that the star is not the one who flies through the air, it is the catcher whose hands are always there to receive them. He said in a film about his trapeze theology:

'if we are to take risks, to be free, in the air in life, we have to know there's a catcher. We have to know that, when we come down from it all, we're going to be caught, we're going to be safe. The great hero is the least visible. Trust the catcher.' [4]

Michael Andrew Ford who wrote a biography of Nouwen's life states:

'The trapeze was a simple, yet powerful metaphor for the spiritual life: it was about letting go and being caught. At one level Nouwen was obviously the flyer who needed to be caught and held – but at another he was very much the catcher in the way in which he received people unconditionally and non-judgmentally, being present to them with a spirit which gave them security and confidence and pointed them to something beyond...Their life-span was an opportunity to express gratitude for the love which had caught them.' [5]

This dual role of being the one caught and being the catcher for others by pointing to God, speaks into the ministry of reconciliation at the heart of being an ambassador. I have been wondering how the various paradoxes in this book would work together. How is it that we have everything we need in the resources of being in union with Christ but, at the same time, we are called to come empty handed and surrender ourselves to God? How do 'process and risk', 'knowledge and mystery', 'experience and faith', all work together? What does it mean to have life in all its fullness given to us by the Spirit, but to be willing to die to oneself to have it? It seems to me that this is a juxtaposition of opposites and yet, when I saw the rope swing next to the end of the bridge in my imagination, I realise this one image encapsulates it all.

Nouwen used the trapeze image to help those who were bereaved with the theology of life after death. He says:

'Dying is trusting in the catcher. To care for the dying is to say, 'Don't be afraid. Remember that you are the beloved child of God. He will be there when you make your long jump. Don't try to grab him: he will grab you. Just stretch out your arms and hands and trust, trust, trust.' [6]

Jesus says to His disciples that whoever loses their life for His sake will find it. [7] This is not having a death-wish in the way that some might interpret it to be, it is the willingness to lay down what we are holding onto, to choose risk rather than security, because we already have that union in Him. As God gives us revelation of His truth, we experience small deaths within us. They are those things that we believed as true, which are now revealed in the light of God as something else. We cannot rely on them in the way we did before because their nature has been exposed. We must let go and let God draw us closer to Him and His truth.

The rope swing does not symbolise for me a time of recreation and fun just to give me a break on the journey. I'm not invited to relax and swing on it while I await another delivery of bricks for my bridge building. This is because I am not the thrill-seeking type. I don't do rollercoasters.

Some years ago, we went as a family on a trip to

Universal Studios in The States. We went on a simulator ride which I thought I would be okay with. The seats that we were secured in, moved, tilted, and experienced relatively small drops, while we watched the film in front of us. Despite the amazing technology and computer-generated graphics on the ride, I did not enjoy it and I still experienced a horrible migraine afterwards.

I took the picture of the rope swing at the end of the bridge to God and practised the two-way journaling that has become part of our communication. I knew that the rope swing represented a choice of direction. There is always a choice with love. I could stay on the bridge, or I could take hold of the rope and swing out to wherever it would take me, knowing that at some point I probably have to let go in the hope and expectation that I will be caught by The Catcher. In the response to my question of what to do, I felt that God said:

'I know you will be anxious, but some situations are like Gordian Knots; you just have to be brave and slice through them. The more you dither and attempt to unravel them, the more frustrated and entangled you become. See it plainly for what it is and gather your courage. The next adventure is where the rope swing takes you.'

All of this was said to the woman who didn't even like going high on a swing when she was a child. It's a big ask but I know that the choice is already taken. I cannot analyse or deconstruct it, arguing for and against and weighing up the various merits of each course of action. That way will only lead to procrastination and getting stuck in more anxiety. I knew instinctively that, as Susan Jeffers would say in her book, that I needed to *Feel the fear and do it anyway.* She states:

'All you have to do to diminish your fear is to develop more trust in your ability to handle whatever comes your way!' [8]

Although this was sound advice, the words *All you have to do* seemed another big ask, but perhaps that is the point. It is the fear of failing, of looking stupid, or being rejected, that gets in the way of most great endeavours. God was reminding me that the decision before me was like a Gordian Knot. It can't be teased out to a clear conclusion. It requires the sword of truth to slice through it. It requires courage and trust in Him that He will indeed catch me whenever I let go.

So that's the question at the end of this book. Am I ready and willing to take the risk and let go?

And if you too, hear the call to be an ambassador for Christ, what will you do?

NOTES

Prologue

1. The Oxford Encyclopedic English Dictionary

Introduction - Building A Bridge As We Walk Across It

1. Susan Beaumont *'How to Lead When You Don't Know Where You're Going'* (2019) Rowman & Littlefield Publishers (p. 7)
2. Ibid. (p.2)
3. Mandy Carr *'The Beach – A Journey Through Pain with the God of Play'* (2021) Amazon Publishing (p. 242)
4. 2 Corinthians 5: 20-21
5. Tom Wright *'Paul for Everyone – 2 Corinthians'* (2003) SPCK (p.65)
6. Ibid. (p.8)
7. Peter Scazzero with Warren Bird *'The Emotionally Healthy Church – A Strategy for Discipleship that Actually Changes Lives.'* (2003) Zondervan (p.49-50)

1. In Search Of The Kingdom

1. Genesis 17
2. Exodus 12-14
3. Exodus 13: 21
4. Exodus 16:14
5. Exodus 19-20 and 24
6. Richard A. Horsley *'Jesus and Empire – The Kingdom of God and the New World Disorder'* (2003) Augsburg Fortress (p.42)
7. 1 Samuel 8: 5

8. 1 Samuel 15

9. Donald B. Kraybill *'The Upside-Down Kingdom'* (2003) Herald Press (p. 47)

10. For example: Psalms 2, 26, 22, 34, 69,1 10; Isaiah 7, 8, 9, 11; Ezekiel 37

11. Donald B. Kraybill *'The Upside-Down Kingdom'* (2003) Herald Press (p. 47)

12. Nick Page *'The Wrong Messiah – The Real Story of Jesus of Nazareth'* (2011) Hodder and Stoughton (p.276)

13. Kenneth E. Bailey *'Jesus Through Middle Easter Eyes – cultural studies in the Gospels'* (2008) SPCK (p.114)

14. Matthew 4: 17; Luke 10: 9

15. Luke 21: 5-36; Matthew 24: 36.

16. Matthew 6: 10

17. Luke 17: 20-21

18. John 3:5; Matthew 6: 33; Mark 9: 47; Matthew 7:21

19. Donald B. Kraybill *'The Upside-Down Kingdom'* (2003) Herald Press (p.18)

20. (2018) XP Publishing

21. Luke 24: 31

22. Phil Mason *'Quantum Glory: The Science of Heaven Invading Earth'* (2018) XP Publishing (p.87)

23. Hebrews 6:19; Hebrews 10: 20;

24. 2 Corinthians 3: 16-18;

25. Phil Mason *'Quantum Glory: The Science of Heaven Invading Earth'* (2018) XP Publishing (p.108)

26. Rob Bell *'What we talk about when we talk about God'* (2013) Collins (p.41)

27. Ibid. (p. 33)

28. John Polkinghorne *'Quantum Physics and Theology: An Unexpected Kinship'* (2007) SPCK (p.1)

29. Bill Johnson *'When Heaven Invades Earth – A Practical Guide to a Life of Miracles'* (2003) Treasure House (p.58)

2. Dethroning Caesar

1. https://www.collinsdictionary.com/dictionary/english/kingdom

2. Richard A. Horsley *'Jesus and Empire – The Kingdom of God and*

the *New World Disorder'* (2003) Fortress Press. (p.134)
3. Romans 10:9
4. Matthew 18: 3-4
5. Walter Wink *'Engaging the Powers – Discernment and Resistance in a World of Domination'* (1992) Fortress Press (p.110)
6. Colossians 1: 16; 2: 15; Ephesians 2: 2; 3: 10; 6: 12; 1 Peter 3: 22
7. Walter Wink *'Engaging the Powers – Discernment and Resistance in a World of Domination'* (1992) Fortress Press (p. 6)
8. Ibid. p. 9
9. Proverbs 11: 2; Romans 12: 26; Colossians 3: 20; Philippians 2:3; Ephesians 4: 2; James 4: 10
10. Mark 9: 35
11. Walter Wink *'Engaging the Powers – Discernment and Resistance in a World of Domination'* (1992) Fortress Press (p. 301)
12. Tom Wright *'The Day the Revolution Began – Rethinking the meaning of Jesus' Crucifixion'* (2016) SPCK (p.254)
13. Ibid. p.84
14. Ibid.p. 132

3. Union

1. Matthew 9: 14-17; Mark 2: 18-22; Luke 5: 33-39
2. Judges 6: 12
3. Judges 6: 15
4. Philippians 1: 6
5. Matthew 1:23 quoting Isaiah 7: 14.
6. Samuel Wells *'A Nazareth Manifesto: Being with God'* (2015) Wiley
7. Ibid. p.8
8. Ibid.
9. Ibid. p.10
10. John 15: 4
11. John 17: 22-23
12. Samuel Wells *'A Nazareth Manifesto: Being with God'* (2015) Wiley p. 6
13. Mother Teresa, with Jose-Luis Gonzalez-Balado *'In My Own Words'* (1997) Gramercy Books
14. Heidi Baker with Shara Pradham *'Compelled by Love – How to change the world through the simple power of love in action'*

(2008) Charisma House p. 17-18

15. Samuel Wells *'A Nazareth Manifesto: Being with God'* (2015) Wiley p. 152

16. Ibid. p.154

17. For example: Mark 10: 17-27; John 6: 60-71; Matthew 8: 21-22; Luke 4: 29-9.

18. Romans 6: 1-7

19. Phil Mason *'Quantum Glory: The Science of Heaven Invading Earth'* (2018) XP Publishing (p.64)

20. Luke 17: 20-21

21. Psalm 139: 7-12

4. Relapse

1. Alan Gordon, and Alon Ziv *'The Way Out: The Revolutionary, Scientifically Proven Approach to Heal Chronic Pain'* (2021) : Vermilion (p.142)

2. Ibid. (p. 149)

3. Matthew 6:33; Luke 12: 31

4. Luke 12: 32

5. Matthew 7:11;

6. Pete Carter *'Unwrapping Lazarus – free to live as God intended'* (2013) River Publishing (p.145)

7. Acts 4: 13

8. Hebrews 12: 1-2

5. Partners in Borrowed Shoes

1. www.marilynsimandle.com

2. Matthew 18: 3; Mark 10: 15.

3. Heidi Baker *'Birthing the Miraculous: The Power of Personal Encounters with God to Change Your Life and the World'* (2014) Charisma House (p.85)

4. Melody Beattie *'Co-dependent No More – How to stop controlling others and start caring for yourself'* (2018) Hazelden Publishing

5. Ibid.

6. Unfinished Business

1. John 15: v.2
2. Kris Vallotton *'Spiritual Intelligence : The Art of Thinking Like God'* (2020) Chosen Books (p. 60)
3. Mark 2: 21-11
4. Bill Johnson *'Open Heavens – Position Yourself to Encounter the God of Revival'* (2021) Destiny Image (p.121)
5. Romans 5: 3-5
6. Romans 3: 23
7. For example: John 3: 16-18; Romans 5: 5-9; Romans 6: 23; 1 Corinthians 15: 1-4; Hebrews 1: 2-3; 1 Peter 2: 22-25; 1 John 2: 1-2
8. 1 Corinthians 2: 16
9. Proverbs 13: 12
10. Bill Johnson *'The Supernatural Power of a Transformed Mind – Access to a life of Miracles'* (2005) Destiny Image (p.152)
11. This two-way Journaling practice of listening to God is outlined by Mark Virkler. Basing this on Habbakuk 1-2, he suggests that we first quieten the mind down, then visualise Jesus, fixing our eyes on Him with our Godly imagination. Then we yield to an inner flow and write down what we hear, setting aside reason, logic and doubt and just tuning into the flow state.
12. Bill Johnson; Kris Vallotton *'The Supernatural Ways of Royalty: Discovering Your Rights and Privileges of Being a Son or Daughter of God'* (2017) Destiny Image (p.55)
13. Nadia Bolz-Weber *'Shameless: a sexual reformation'* (2019) Canterbury Press Norwich
14. Shawn Bolz *'Through the Eyes of Love'* (2019) Thomas Nelson (p.81)

7. Offence

1. John Bevere *'The Bait of Satan: Living Free from the Deadly Trap of Offense'* (2014) Charisma House (p.60)
2. Heidi Baker *'Birthing the Miraculous: The Power of Personal Encounters with God to Change Your Life and the World'* (2014) Charisma House (p.132)

3. Genesis 37, 39-40.
4. Genesis 41: 51-2
5. Exodus 1: 8-20; 3: 7.
6. Genesis 21: 17
7. Genesis 4:10
8. Psalm 34:17; 10:18; 120:1; 130:1.
9. Luke 4: 18-21
10. Jonah 4
11. Luke 24: 34
12. Matthew 12: 14; Matthew 20: 18-19; Mark 10: 33; Luke 18: 31-33; Luke 22: 1-6; John 11: 45-57.
13. Matthew 27:24
14. Nadia Bolz-Weber *'Accidental Saints'* (2015) Canterbury Press (p.110)
15. William Shakespeare, *Macbeth* Act III Scene 4
16. Matthew 5: 43-8; Luke 6: 28, 35.
17. Genesis 1: 27
18. Matthew 10:16
19. John Bevere *'The Bait of Satan: Living Free from the Deadly Trap of Offense'* (2014) Charisma House (p.11)
20. https://www.buzzsprout.com/1902128/10310229 Spiritual Soundings Episode 11: Interview Special with the Very Reverend Professor Martyn Percy. March 24 2022. Lorraine Cavanagh.
21. John Bevere *'The Bait of Satan: Living Free from the Deadly Trap of Offense'* (2014) Charisma House (p.60)
22. Matthew 7: 5
23. Walter Wink *'Engaging the Powers – Discernment and Resistance in a World of Domination'* (1992) Fortress Press (p. 271)
24. Ibid. (p. 270)
25. Ibid (p.68)
26. Walter Wink *'Engaging the Powers – Discernment and Resistance in a World of Domination'* (1992) Fortress Press (p. 267)
27. Nadia Bolz-Weber *'Shameless: A sexual reformation'* (2019) Canterbury Press Norwich.

8. Blessing

1. Russ Parker *'Rediscovering the ministry of blessing'* (2014) SPCK (p.99)
2. Proverbs 26: 2
3. Walter Wink *'Engaging the Powers – Discernment and Resistance in a world of Domination'* (1992) Fortress Press (p.195)
4. Romans 12: 21
5. Romans 12: 20 quoting Proverbs 25: 21-22
6. https://www.prayerfoundation.org
7. Roy Godwin and Dave Roberts *'The Grace Outpouring – Blessing Others Through Prayer : The amazing story of God's work at Ffald-y-Brenin'* (2008) David C. Cook (p.27)
8. Numbers 6: 22-26
9. Isaiah 55: 11
10. Roy Godwin and Dave Roberts *'The Grace Outpouring – Blessing Others Through Prayer : The amazing story of God's work at Ffald-y-Brenin'* (2008) David C. Cook (p.33)
11. Roy Godwin and Dave Roberts *'The Grace Outpouring – Blessing Others Through Prayer : The amazing story of God's work at Ffald-y-Brenin'* (2008) David C. Cook (p.52)
12. Russ Parker *'Healing Wounded History – reconciling peoples and healing places* (2001) Darton, Longman and Todd (p.8)
13. Matthew 5: 24; Ephesians 4: 32; Colossians 3: 13; Hebrews 12: 14
14. 2 Corinthians 18-21
15. Brian Castle *'Reconciliation – The journey of a lifetime'* (2014) SPCK (p.12)
16. Ibid. (p.13)

9. Course Correction

1. Hebrews 12: 1-2
2. 2 Corinthians 5: 20
3. For example, Proverbs 2: 1-5; John 15: 7, 10; John 11: 40.
4. Luke 6: 38; Galatians 6: 7-8.
5. Philip Yancey *'What's So Amazing About Grace'* (1997) Zondervan (p.25)
6. Luke 15: 11-32

7. Lois Tverberg *'Walking in the Dust of Rabbi Jesus – How the Jewish words of Jesus can change your life'* (2012) Zondervan (p.169)

8. Henri J. M. Nouwen *'The Return of The Prodigal Son – A Story of Homecoming'* (1994) Darton, Longman and Todd (p.36)

9. Lois Tverberg *'Walking in the Dust of Rabbi Jesus – How the Jewish words of Jesus can change your life'* (2012) Zondervan (p.169)

10. Kenneth Bailey's commentary on Luke 15: 11-31 https://www.youtube.com/watch?v=GcYDhDvQaRI

11. Ibid.

12. Luke 15: 17

13. Verse 17 and 19 specifically talk about a 'hired' servant which involves payment for service.

14. Kenneth Bailey's commentary on Luke 15: 11-31 https://www.youtube.com/watch?v=GcYDhDvQaRI

15. Ibid

16. Ibid

17. Luke 15: 5-6

18. Kenneth Bailey's commentary on Luke 15: 11-31 https://www.youtube.com/watch?v=GcYDhDvQaRI

19. v. 22-24;

20. Kenneth E. Bailey *'The Cross and the Prodigal – Luke 15 Through the Eyes of Middle Eastern Peasants'* (2005) InterVarsity Press (p.82)

21. v.30

22. v.31

23. Henri J. M. Nouwen *'The Return of The Prodigal Son – A Story of Homecoming'* (1994) Darton, Longman and Todd (p.108-109)

24. Philippians 2: 6-8

25. Matthew 1:23

26. Hebrews 12: 2

27. Romans 5:8

28. Quoted in Philip Yancey *'What's So Amazing about Grace?'* (1997) Zondervan (p.15)

29. Galatians 5: 7

30. Galatians 5: 1

31. Nadia Bolz-Weber *'Shameless: A sexual reformation'* (2019) Canterbury Press Norwich

32. Romans 6: 1

33. 1 Corinthians 8: 9

34. Kenneth E. Bailey *'Paul Through Mediterranean Eyes - Cultural Studies in 1 Corinthians'* (2011) SPCK (p.291)

35. Barbara Brown Taylor *'An Altar in the World – Finding the sacred beneath our feet'* (2009) Canterbury Press. (p.xvii)

10. Gordian Knots

1. https://www.history.com/

2. Kenneth E. Bailey *'The Cross and the Prodigal – Luke 15 Through the Eyes of Middle Eastern Peasants'* (2005) InterVarsity Press (p.67)

3. Rebecca C. Mandeville *'Rejected, shamed and Blamed: Help and Hope for Adults in the Family Scapegoat Role'* (2020) Independently Published (p.94-95)

4. Ibid. (p.88)

5. Blake K. Healy *'Indestructible : Fight your Spiritual Battles from the Winning Side'* (2020) Charisma House. (p.98)

6. Psalm 139: 23-24

7. Richard Rohr and Mike Morrell *'The Divine Dance – The Trinity and Your Transformation'* (2016) SPCK (p.51)

8. Ibid. p.49

9. Ibid. p.112-3

10. 1 Corinthians 6: 19-20

11. Richard Rohr and Mike Morrell *'The Divine Dance – The Trinity and Your Transformation'* (2016) SPCK (p.113)

12. Matthew 6: 25 -34

13. Luke 2: 51

14. Psalm 46: 10

15. Psalm 46: 2-3

16. Richard Rohr and Mike Morrell *'The Divine Dance – The Trinity and Your Transformation'* (2016) SPCK (p.135)

17. Colossians 1: 15-20

18. John 14: 8-11

19. John 15: 15

11. The Question Of Power

1. Letter to Bishop Mandell Creighton (April 5, 1887) published in *'Historical Essays'* (1907) Eds. J. N. Figgis and R. V. Laurence. Macmillan.

2. Donald B. Kraybill *'The Upside-Down Kingdom'* (2003) Herald Press (p. 52)

3. Philippians 2: 6-8

4. I Corinthians 11: 23-26

5. John 10: 18

6. John 14: 30 (NRSV)

7. C. S. Lewis *'The Lion, The Witch and the Wardrobe'* (1950) published as 'The Complete Chronicles of Narnia' (1989) HarperCollins (p.125)

8. John 18: 10-11;

9. Matthew 26: 52-54

10. Walter Wink *'Engaging the Powers – Discernment and Resistance in a World of Domination'* (1992) Fortress Press (p. 30)

11. Dale W. Brown *'Biblical Pacifism'* (1986) Brethren Press. (ix)quoted in Ibid. p. 216

12. This is discussed at much greater length in the book *'The Beach'*

13. Dennis Linn, Sheila Fabricant Linn, Matthew Linn *'Don't Forgive Too Soon – extending the Two Hands that Heal'* (1997) Paulist Press: (p.21)

14. Ibid. p. 14.

15. Ibid, p. 15 and 18

16. Ibid. 19-20.

17. https://www.theguardian.com/uk/2013/may/27/york-mosque-protest-tea-biscuits

18. I Corinthians 2: 4-5

19. Ian Cowley *'Going Empty-Handed;'* (1996) Monarch Publications (p.20)

20. Thomas a Kempis *'The Imitation of Christ'* (1418) Book 1: Ch 16

21. https://rapecrisis.org.uk/get-informed/statistics-sexual-violence/

22. Danny Silk *'Keep Your Love On! – Connection, Communication & Boundaries'* (2013) Lovingonpurpose.com (p.20 and 25)

12. Communication With HQ

1. Proverbs 24: 5: 'The wise prevail through great power, and those who have knowledge muster their strength.'
2. Kenneth E. Bailey *'The Good Shepherd – A thousand year journey from Psalm 23 to the New Testament'* (2015) SPCK (p. 17)
3. Walter Wink *'Engaging the Powers – Discernment and Resistance in a World of Domination'* (1993) Fortress Press (p. 362-3)
4. L. Newbigin *'The Gospel in a Pluralist Society'* Quoted in Kenneth E. Bailey's *'Jacob and the Prodigal – How Jesus Retold Israel's Story'* (2003) InterVarsity Press
5. Kenneth E. Bailey's *'Jacob and the Prodigal – How Jesus Retold Israel's Story'* (2003) InterVarsity Press (p.38)
6. Caroline Criado Perez *'Invisible Women – exposing Data Bias in a World Designed for Men'* (2019) Vintage (p. xii)
7. Dr. Lisa Oakley and Justin Humphreys *'Escaping the Maze of Spiritual Abuse – Creating Healthy Christian Cultures'* (2019) SPCK (p.45)
8. Available to listen at www.godlymischief.com
9. 1 Corinthians 14: 1
10. Shawn Bolz *'Translating God: hearing God's Voice for Yourself and the World Around You.'* (2015) ICreate Productions (p.167)
11. Shawn Bolz *'Translating God: hearing God's Voice for Yourself and the World Around You.'* (2015) ICreate Productions p.152
12. Mark Virkler *'How to hear God's Voice'* (2006) Destiny Image.
13. Ibid.
14. James W. Goll *'The Scribe : Reviving and Retaining Revelation through Journaling'* (2020) Destiny Image (p.58)
15. Ibid p.38
16. Ibid. (p. 20)

13. Kingdom Values

1. Heidi and Rolland Baker *'Learning to love: passion and compassion: the essence of the Gospel'* (2012) River publishing and Media Ltd.
2. Ibid. (p.24)
3. 1 John 4: 7-21; 1 Corinthians 13

4. Heidi and Rolland Baker *'Learning to love: passion and compassion: the essence of the Gospel'* (2012) River publishing and Media Ltd. (p.19)
5. Vincent J. Donovan *'Christianity Rediscovered'* (2005) – 25th Anniversary Edition Orbis Books (p.1)
6. Ibid. p.156
7. Ibid. p. 151-2
8. Ibid. xiii
9. Ibid. p. 143
10. Elaine Storkey *'Scars Across Humanity – Understanding and Overcoming Violence Against Women'* (2015) SPCK (p.74)
11. Luke 14: 1-11
12. Verse 11
13. Matthew 18: 1-5
14. Mark 10: 35-45
15. Matthew 20:23
16. Matthew 20:26-27; Mark 10: 43-44.
17. Danny Silk *'Keep Your Love On! Connection, Communication and Boundaries'* (2013) lovingonpurpose.com (p.66)
18. Ibid. (p.67)
19. Luke 7: 36-50
20. Heidi and Roland Baker *'Learning to love: passion and compassion: the essence of the Gospel'* (2012) River publishing and Media Ltd.
21. Shawn Bolz *'Through the Eyes of Love'* (2019) Thomas Nelson (p.28)
22. Donald B. Kraybill *'The Upside-Down Kingdom'* (2003) Herald Press (p. 17)
23. I Corinthians 13: 1
24. I Corinthians 13: 13

14. The Practice Of Proclamation

1. Kenneth E. Bailey *'Jesus Through Middle Easter Eyes – Cultural Studies in the Gospels'* (2008) SPCK (p.147)
2. Ibid. (p.149) Qumran 4Q278, 521.
3. Ibid. (p.156)
4. Leviticus 25: 8-55
5. Donald B. Kraybill *'The Upside-Down Kingdom'* (2003) Herald

press (p.90)

6. Luke 4: 21
7. Joachim Jeremias and Ibn al-Tayyib as quoted in Bailey's *'Jesus through Middle Easter Eyes'* (p.151)
8. Ibid (p.162)
9. Luke 4: 26-27 the widow in Zarephath in Sidon in Elijah's time, and during the time of Elisha, Naaman the Syrian was healed from leprosy.
10. Ibid. (p.168)
11. Samuel Wells *'A Nazareth Manifesto: Being with God'* (2015) Wiley (p.151)
12. John 10: 16
13. Romans 11
14. John 19: 28-30
15. Mark 2: 19-20 and Matthew 25:1-13; John 3: 29; Ephesians 5: 25-27, Revelation 19:7-9, 21:1-2.
16. *The Passion Translation* (2018) Broad Street Publishing Group
17. Ibid.
18. Luke 12:32
19. Jane Hamon *'Declarations for Breakthrough'* (2021) Chosen Books p. 13.
20. Ibid. (p.15)
21. Ibid (p.42)
22. Ibid (p.20)
23. Isaiah 55: 11

15. Re-Wiring Required

1. Shawn Bolz *'Translating God: Hearing God's Voice for Yourself and the World Around You.'* (2015) ICreate Productions (p.89)
2. Liturgy of Baptism – Presentation of the Candidates. *'Common Worship – Services and Prayers for the Church of England* (2000) Church House Publishing
3. https://dictionary.cambridge.org/dictionary/english/indoc-trination
4. Genesis 2: 9, 17
5. Deuteronomy 30: 19
6. Dr. Caroline Leaf *'Switch On Your Brain -The Key to Peak Happiness, Thinking and Health'* (2013) Baker Books

7. Ibid. (p.47)
8. Romans 12: 2
9. John 16: 13
10. 1 Peter 2: 8 from Isaiah 8: 14
11. Matthew 16: 24-26; Mark 8: 34; Luke 9: 23
12. John 3
13. Matthew 8: 5-13
14. Matthew 27: 57-60
15. Luke 24:10
16. Luke 8: 3
17. Donald B. Kraybill *'The Upside-Down Kingdom'* (2003) Herald Press (p. 254)
18. Heidi and Rolland Baker *'Learning to Love: Passion and compassion: the essence of the Gospel'* (2012) River publishing and Media Ltd. (p.117)
19. 1 Corinthians 2:16
20. Tom Wright *'Paul for Everyone – 1 Corinthians'* (2003) SPCK (p.31)
21. Dr. Caroline Leaf *'Switch On Your Brain -The Key to Peak Happiness, Thinking and Health'* (2013) Baker Books (p.67)
22. Ibid. (p.128)
23. Ibid. (p.140)
24. Ibid. (p.150)
25. Philippians 4: 8
26. Rick Hanson *'Hardwiring Happiness: The New Brain Science of Contentment, Calm and Confidence'*. (2013) Penguin Random House quoted in Richard Rohr with Mike Morrel *'The Divine Dance – the Trinity and your Transformation'* (2016) SPCK (p.116)
27. Ibid.(p.116)
28. Donald B. Kraybill *'The Upside-Down Kingdom'* (2003) Herald Press (p.255-6)
29. 2 Corinthians 3: 18 (NRSV)

16. The Seal Of The Lamb

1. Canon C12: https://www.churchofengland.org/about/leadership-and-governance/legal-services/canons-church-england/section-c
2. Ministers, their ordinations, functions and charge. C10: Of

admission and institution/ 6. https://www.churchofeng-land.org/about/leadership-and-governance/legal-services/canons-church-england/section-c

3. https://blogs.oxford.anglican.org/the-cure-of-souls/
4. Leviticus 4: 32-35
5. John 1: 29
6. 1 Peter 18-19
7. Revelation 5-7
8. Revelation 5: 12
9. *'The Image of Christ: The Catalogue of the exhibition Seeing Salvation'*(2000) National Gallery Company Ltd. (p. 36)
10. The Bound Lamb (Agnus Dei) about 1635-1640 https://www.-museodelprado.es/en/the-collection/art-work/agnus-dei/795b841a-ec81-4d10-bd8b-0c7a870e327b
11. Jane Hamon *'Declarations for Breakthrough – Agreeing with the Voice of God'* (2021) Chosen Books (p.153)
12. Songwriters: Michael W. Smith / Jason Ingram / Scott Ligert-wood / Brooke Ligertwood
    Agnus Dei / King of Kings lyrics © Sony/atv Milene Music, So Essential Tunes, Hillsong Music Publishing Australia. Source: Musixmatch

17. Working From Rest

1. Psalm 46: 10
2. Dr. Caroline Leaf *'Switch On Your Brain: The Key to Peak Happiness, Thinking and Health'* (2013) Baker Books (p.79)
3. Ibid. (p.82)
4. Ibid. (p 83 and 85)
5. 1 Peter 4: 8
6. Jeremy Myers *'The Death and Resurrection of the Church: A Call for the Church to Die so it can Rise Again'* (2013) Redeeming Press (p.68)
7. Rolland and Heidi Baker *'Learning to Love: Passion and compassion: the essence of the Gospel'* (2012) River publishing Media Ltd. (p. 44)
8. Martyn Percy *'The Humble Church – renewing the body of Christ'* (2021) Canterbury Press (p.23)
9. Ibid. (p.70)

10. Prophetic Word from 17.11.22
11. Rolland and Heidi Baker *'Learning to Love: Passion and compassion: the essence of the Gospel'* (2012) River publishing Media Ltd (p.60)
12. Ibid. (p. 74)
13. Mark 4: 26-29
14. John 10: 10
15. John 7: 38
16. John 12: 24-25
17. John 14: 6
18. Matthew 27: 51

18. Living Inside Out For Others

1. https://my.salvos.org.au/news/2014/06/23/making-others-the-focus-for-one-week/
2. E. Randolph Richards and Brandon J. O'Brien *'Misreading Scripture with Western Eyes – Removing Cultural Blinders to better Understand the Bible'* (2012) IVP Books (p.207)
3. Richard A. Horsley *'Jesus and Empire – The Kingdom of God and the New World Disorder'* (2003) Fortress Press. (p. 7)
4. E. Randolph Richards and Brandon J. O'Brien *'Misreading Scripture with Western Eyes – Removing Cultural Blinders to better Understand the Bible'* (2012) IVP Books (p. 195)
5. Martyn Percy *'The Humble Church – Renewing the Body of Christ'* (2021) Canterbury Press (p. 69)
6. From the Declaration of Assent from the Church of England Canon Law. *This is made by deacons, priests and bishops of the Church of England when they are ordained and on each occasion when they take up a new appointment (Canon C 15).* https://www.churchofengland.org/prayer-and-worship/worship-texts-and-resources/common-worship/ministry/declaration-assent
7. Henri J. M. Nouwen *'In the Name of Jesus – Reflections on Christian Leadership'* (1989) Darton, Longman and Todd (p.71)
8. Jeremy Myers *'The Death and Resurrection of The Church: A Call for the Church to Die so it Can Rise Again'* (2013) Redeeming Press (p. 44)
9. Matthew 6: 33
10. Matthew 16: 18-19

11. Pete Carter *'Unwrapping Lazarus – free to live as God intended'* (2013) River Publishing (p.57)
12. Deuteronomy 6: 4-5 Shema Yisrael
13. Leviticus 19: 18
14. Mark 12: 28-33
15. John 15: 12-13
16. Matthew 7: 13-14
17. Luke 10: 25-37; Matthew 8: 5-13; Luke 7: 36-50; John 20: 11-18
18. 1 John 4: 7-21
19. Rolland and Heidi Baker *'Learning to Love: Passion and Compassion: the essence of the Gospel'* (2012) River Publishing Media Ltd. (p.143)
20. Ibid. (p.144 and 180)
21. 2 Corinthians 4: 7
22. Rolland and Heidi Baker *'Learning to Love: Passion and Compassion: the essence of the Gospel'* (2012) River Publishing Media Ltd (p.180)

Epilogue - The Rope Swing At The End Of The Bridge

1. Matthew 10; Luke 9: 1-6; Luke 10: 1-23;
2. Matthew 10: 8
3. William Shakespeare's *Hamlet* Act III scene I
4. From *Angels over the Net* (The Company, Spark Productions 1995) Quoted in Michael Andrew Ford *'Wounded Prophet – A Portrait of Henri J.M. Nouwen'* (2006) Darton, Longman and Todd Ltd (p.34)
5. Michael Andrew Ford *'Wounded Prophet – A Portrait of Henri J.M. Nouwen'* (2006) Darton, Longman and Todd Ltd (p.224)
6. Ibid. (p.224)
7. Matthew 16: 25; Mark 8: 35; Luke9: 24; 17: 33; John 12: 25
8. Susan Jeffers *'Feel the fear and do it anyway'* (2007) Vermilion (p.14)

ACKNOWLEDGMENTS

I am hugely grateful for all those who have helped me with this book. I would like to thank Canon Jean Kerr for her wisdom, insightful comments, challenges, and discussion points. Thank you also Jean for kindly agreeing to write the foreword for me. I also am grateful for the input from Canon Gordon Oliver whose thoughtful critiques and reflections kept me on the straight and narrow or, at least helped me to see things from a different perspective. To Linda Walker for designing and producing a fabulous image for the cover. For Patrick Carr for his incredible patience in going through the manuscript, offering feedback, and correcting the worst elements of my grammatical style. I'm sure we haven't picked up all my misdemeanours, but I hope we've spotted and corrected the worst offenders. Thank you to Judith Boarer for being a sounding board for the story, and for discussions over lunch. Thank you to Patrick, Matthew and Charlie, for just being the best and making sure I never take myself too seriously.

ABOUT THE AUTHOR

Mandy Carr is a writer, film-maker and Anglican Priest with a passion for the prophetic. *The Ambassador* is her second book and the sequel to *The Beach*. Mandy lives in Kent with her family.

Printed in Great Britain
by Amazon

23694218R00165